Michel Tournier

Michel Tournier

Le Coq de bruyère

Walter Redfern

Madison • Teaneck
Fairleigh Dickinson University Press
London: Associated University Presses

© 1996 by Associated University Presses, Inc.

All rights reserved. Authorization to photocopy items for internal or personal use, or the internal or personal use of specific clients, is granted by the copyright owner, provided that a base fee of $10.00, plus eight cents per page, per copy is paid directly to the Copyright Clearance Center, 222 Rosewood Drive, Danvers, Massachusetts 01923. [0-8386-3627-6/96 $10.00+8¢ pp, pc.]

Associated University Presses
440 Forsgate Drive
Cranbury, NJ 08512

Associated University Presses
25 Sicilian Avenue
London WC1A 2QH, England

Associated University Presses
P.O. Box 338, Port Credit
Mississauga, Ontario
Canada L5G 4L8

The paper used in this publication meets the requirements of the American National Standard for Permanence of Paper for Printed Library Materials Z39.48-1984.

Library of Congress Cataloging-in-Publication Data

Redfern, W. D.
  Michel Tournier, Le coq de bruyère / Walter Redfern.
    p. cm.
  Includes bibliographical references and index.
  ISBN 0-8386-3627-6 (alk. paper)
  1. Tournier, Michel. Coq de bruyère. I. Title.
PQ2680.O83C637   1996
843'.914—dc20   95-32323
                                                            CIP

PRINTED IN THE UNITED STATES OF AMERICA

For My Nuclear Family

Contents

List of Abbreviations	9
Preface	11
1. The Founding Myth: "La Famille Adam"	17
2. Closure of the Myth: "La Fin de Robinson Crusoé"	22
3. Creation of Legend: "La Mère Noël"	24
4. The Good Initiation: "Amandine ou les deux jardins"	26
5. Child Father to Man: "La Fugue du petit Poucet"	32
6. Sex and Confusion: "Tupik"	37
7. The Optative Mode: "Que ma joie demeure"	42
8. Purifying Laughter: "Le Nain rouge"	46
9. Radio Daze and Imperishable Myth: "Tristan Vox"	55
10. Photographic Fetishism: "Les Suaires de Véronique"	62
11. Something about Nothing: "La Jeune Fille et la mort"	73
12. The Fetish of Not Seeing: "Le Coq de bruyère"	89
13. Cain and Abel Revisited: "L'Aire du Muguet"	96
14. The Virtues of Perversion: "Le Fétichiste"	101
15. The Play of Words	111
Conclusions	118
Notes	122
Bibliography	132
Index	133

Abbreviations

Stories in *Le Coq de bruyère*

FA: "La Famille Adam"
FRC: "La Fin de Robinson Crusoé"
MN: "La Mère Noël"
A: "Amandine ou les deux jardins"
FPP: "La Fugue du petit Poucet"
T: "Tupik"
QMJD: "Que ma joie demeure"
NR: "Le Nain rouge"
TV: "Tristan Vox"
SV: "Les Suaires de Véronique"
JFM: "La Jeune Fille et la mort"
CB: "Le Coq de bruyère"
AM: "L'Aire du Muguet"
F: "Le Fétichiste"

Other Texts

CM: *Le Crépuscule des masques*
CS: *Des Clefs et des serrures*
GO: *La Goutte d'or*
M: *Les Météores*
RA: *Le Roi des aulnes*
VD: *Vues de dos*
VI: *Le Vagabond immobile*
VLP: *Vendredi ou les limbes du Pacifique*
VP: *Le Vent Paraclet*
VV: *Le Vol du vampire*

Preface

> Now we are going to begin. When we have come to the end
> we shall know a great deal more than we do now.
> —Hans Christian Andersen

NOWADAYS, Michel Tournier tends to define himself as a storyteller, not as a novelist. His latest fictional work, *Le Médianoche amoureux*, is a roughly connected set of *contes*. Indeed, he has declared: "Mes romans sont des enchevêtrements de contes."[1] He has long been fascinated by the oriental tradition of tales, typified by the *Thousand and One Nights*. It is fitting to view *Le Coq de bruyère*, a collection of *contes* and *nouvelles*, as a microcosm of Tournier's whole *oeuvre*, or, to use a favorite word of his: *un creuset*, a melting pot or crucible. (The root of "crucible," *crux*, signifies both pointedness and pain). Just as in "Le Nain rouge" in this collection the dwarf's-eye perspective provides a startlingly different slant on human affairs, so a study of Tournier's short stories can illuminate the jumbo fictions for which he is so far better known. These stories pick up on, vary, or extend themes in the previous three full-length novels. After *Le Coq de bruyère*, Tournier goes off in what many find less satisfying directions: *Gaspard, Melchior et Balthazar*, *Gilles et Jeanne*, *La Goutte d'or*, *Le Médianoche amoureux*. As well as featuring several initiation stories, *Le Coq de bruyère* is initiatory, or at least points-switching, in itself. One enforced advantage for him in the short text is that he cannot there cross-thread umpteen themes as in his novels, but must concentrate on fewer. To the question how he is inspired to write, Tournier replied: "Il me faut toujours, hélas, de très grands sujets. Je ne suis pas un intimiste."[2] Even in the short story, Tournier thinks big.

Le Coq de bruyère has magnetized much less critical attention than his other fictions. Undoubtedly he has in it much less room to sprawl and indulge himself, but on the other hand his worst and best qualities stand out more nakedly. All of its stories open up something: a mystery, a can of worms, the imagination, our powers of empathy or compassion. Tournier aims to *enlarge* us (that is: expand and release us).

He claims to distinguish between *un conte* and *une nouvelle*, though the French tradition itself, refreshingly for once, has always been fairly slackly taxonomic in this area. *Nouvelle*, for him, retains its connections with *les nouvelles*. It is principally realistic in intention and has to do with the observable and recordable world; its tone is mostly bleak. A *conte*, on the contrary, is

> un milieu translucide, mais non transparent, comme une épaisseur glauque dans laquelle le lecteur voit se dessiner des figures qu'il ne parvient jamais à saisir tout à fait. (VV, p. 40)

This distinguo suggests that the reader may look into a *conte* but not see totally through it; some mystery remains. *Contes* play upon the less rational fears and desires of readers:

> Un phénomène de souvenir vague et insaisissable, exactement de réminiscence—laquelle selon Joubert est "comme l'ombre du souvenir." Nous retrouvons ici notre fantôme. (VV, p. 42)

This suggests an intertextuality, or a plagiarism, of memory. Different psyches meet up in a mythic rendez-vous.

Myths are multi-layered. This richness explains why they are so frequently recycled. For his part, Tournier often appropriates, diverts, or perverts old myths for the needs of his causes. He wants readers to rediscover, to update, to make relevant to their own times and preoccupations, stories that we already know, or think we know: Adam and Eve, Cain and Abel, Robinson Crusoe, Tom Thumb, Tristan and Iseult, St. Veronica. At first glance, some of these stories are "kids' stuff." Others are "adult" literature. Taken as a whole, they make us question such lazy-minded categorizations. Notoriously, many children's stories were sanitized in the eighteenth and nineteenth centuries by collectors and rewriters. As a result, a curious innuendo often pervades them. If it is true that in Perrault's asides and the morals appended to the stories, he speaks as if he were winking at the adults over the heads of children,[3] Tournier in his aims to enter into complicity with both.

A born fabulator and pedagogue ("On ne peut fabuler sans enseigner")(*VV*, p. 40), Tournier is a self-mythologizer. He arranges his biography, in his accounts of it, to give it the shape, the interconnectedness and the special logic, the premonitions, epiphanies and fulfillments, characteristic of his fictions. His most reliably true confession concerns his humor:

> J'espère que l'humour est partout sensible dans tout ce que j'écris. Sinon, tant pis pour moi. L'humour que je vise ébranle en profondeur tout l'édifice de nos idées, conventions, règles du jeu, etc. . . . C'est un humour qui aggrave le propos au lieu de l'alléger. Sa formule pourrait être: plus je ris, moins je plaisante.[4]

In the blurb to *Le Vent Paraclet*, he prays to the Holy Ghost for the three crucial qualities: "la subtilité, le faste et la drôlerie." Though he wobbles at times, and then sees humor limited to destructive purposes, he recovers in time to add celebration (see *VP*, pp. 196, 204, and *VV*, p. 255).

Although the very idea of eclecticism enrages *dernier cri* critics, choosers are in fact not beggars. Tournier himself is a professed magpie. Why should not his reader be, too? Diamond cut diamond, "à bon chat bon rat." Seeking to interpret Gide, Tournier said:

> Essayer sur lui un trousseau de clefs binaires qui, croyons-nous, tempérées par ce qu'il faut de scepticisme et d'esprit ludique, peuvent contribuer à éclairer l'auteur de l'*Immoraliste*. (*VV*, p. 219)

Note the qualifying remark, the let-out or sanity clause. Indeed, the whole prospect of a systematic approach comes perilously close to self-cancellation: "La dichotomie ne doit pas être maniée comme une hache de bûcheron, mais nuancée au contraire, jusqu'à l'effacement" (*VV*, p. 218). I feel about as scientific, in my study of Tournier, as that other intuitive delver, the etymologist. Above all, we should remember Todorov's reminder: "On n'a pas à s'enfermer dans l'opposition stérile et factice du jeu et du sérieux."[5]

When I tried to demarcate and redistribute the stories along thematic lines, I failed. There is in them so much cross-referencing, reprises, theme-and-variations. It seemed best therefore to stick with Tournier's own sequencing rather than try to extrapolate artificial clusters. Even his distinguo between *nouvelle* and *conte* is far too fluid for use as a classifying device. All I feel assured about saying in general, umbrella terms is that all of the stories in *Le Coq de bruyère* have some form of binary structure, but also some overlap between the two camps or worlds on display. The chief recurrent themes are: initiation (transformations, quests, rituals); marginality; perversion/monstrosity; sexuality and gender; and humor. When asked why he called the whole book after one of its stories (and the English translation, as a come-on, selected *The Fetishist* as a title), Tournier replied simply that it was the longest story in the collection. If this title does not even begin to cover the spread of the fourteen texts, the collection as a whole does feature obsessive themes, and twists on themes (as in Bach's *Art of the Fugue*). Here, Tournier tries out not only numerous ideas, but also various narrative methods, from the pseudo-folksy to the ultra-blasé, from child to old man.

Tournier, who dubbed his younger self "this little metaphysical Tarzan," is disputably the novel lord of the hexagonal jungle. He freely (on photos, at least) bares his chest. Surely, however, he is too irremediably sophisticated to go native. Besides, known as a champion of philosophy, he would be an egghead apeman.

Seeing *Le Coq de bruyère* as a *multum in parvo* of his total work, I have not hesitated to throw bridges between these stories and his other writings at every apt opportunity.

* * *

Chapters 9 and 11 appeared in different form in *French Cultural Studies* and *Journal of European Studies*. I am grateful to the editors, Professors Brian Rigby and John Flower, and to the printer, Richard Sadler of Alpha Academic, for permission to reuse this material.

Michel Tournier

1
The Founding Myth: "La Famille Adam"

> You think Oedipus had a problem—Adam was Eve's mother.
> —Graffito on construction wall, Philadelphia, 1969

LOGICALLY enough, this first story in the collection rewrites Genesis, the founding story of the Judeo-Christian tradition. A rewriting of Holy Writ, it is humorous and pointed. Throughout, God is credited with human-all-too-human attributes: vanity, irascibility, favoritism. Inevitably, the story begins "Au commencement." Tournier has substituted himself for the supreme dictator, God. Tournier's version of God is a narcissist. He plagiarizes himself by creating man in his own image. So at the outset lies the original paradox: creation and imitation were co-instantaneous. This is of course equally true of authors, those little gods. Even when seeking to be original, they are heavily in hock to predecessors.[1]

Tournier reworks to his taste the creation myth. The true Fall was the split-up into three of a previously and marvellously self-contained entity. The Platonic myth of severance is rampant in Tournier's work. His God is unisex, which is not news to today's feminists, to ancient glosses on the Bible which made much of the fact that the very word *Jehovah* comes from roots both masculine and feminine, and to the long Gnostic tradition of an androgynous Adam, God, and soul.[2] Though *sex* derives as probably as not from *secare*, to cut, such traditions refuse to see sex as a phenomenon of separation and opt for dual entities. The androgyne is a figure of approximation in two senses: a near-miss and a bringing-together. As Tournier views the polarization of the sexes as the root cause of myriad problems for humanity, a bisexual God fits his bill.

Tournier is a nonchalant borrower. He improves on Plato, whose

Androgyne was a true, and hideous, monster: globular, one trunk, one head, two faces, two sexes, four arms, and four legs.[3] Tournier's version is more beautiful: a standard human shape with the physical attributes of both genders. Plato's hybrid carries in embryonic form, programmed, the future split. This outcome is not nearly so predetermined in Tournier's, so that the eventual breakup is much more traumatic. Twinhood, the dominant theme of *Les Météores,* provides in Tournier's general compensatory scheme of things a counterbalance to such cleavages, for twins are at their origin two-in-one, lying head-to-tail in the womb. Tournier would seem to prefer that humankind perpetuate itself by parthenogenesis or self-fecundation (the Holy Ghost cannot be everywhere): "Un serpent se mordant la queue est la figure de cette érotique close sur elle-même, sans perte ni bavure" (*VLP*, p. 12). We are, for Tournier, self-begetters.

In *La Famille Adam,* then, God conveniently sports both penis and vagina, as does his mirror image, Adam. This original copy could thus store the former organ in the latter when walking or running, like a knife in a scabbard (an ancient erotic emblem in many cultures). Splendidly self-contained, Adam could have impregnated himself. He has the best of both worlds. Bolshy by nature, however, Adam lets his virile side predominate, that wants to keep on the move and be forever ready for combat. In order to settle Adam down, God creates Eden with a view to increasing his progeny. Initially Adam refuses to acquiesce, while recognizing his bipartite nature: sedentary and nomadic. God therefore waits for Adam to fall asleep (as in the Bible), and then (as not) he subtracts the female parts from bisexual Adam and inserts them into another "man" made from the soil of Paradise: Woman is created. Stripped of his female half, Adam is now fully male. When God introduces Eve to him as his "other half," Adam responds solipsistically: "Comme je suis beau," which God then corrects to the right grammatical gender in the new dispensation: "Comme elle est belle" (*FA*, pp. 13–14). The woman *is* the better half.

The major difference between Tournier's tale and the Genesis myth is that Tournier's offers no explanation as to why Adam and Eve come to be expelled from Eden. The Fall is traditionally blamed on Eve's insatiable curiosity and vulnerability to the serpent's flattering wiles. Tournier very clearly wants to valorize

Woman and devalue Man. In the orthodox telling, the Fall starts off human evolution. While grateful for the emphasis of the eminent geneticist, François Jacob, on the role of chance, games and *bricolage* in evolution, Tournier persists in preferring the Genesis version of mankind as God's self-portrait as richer in meaning than evolutionary theory (nature experimenting with itself).[4] In other words, Tournier dislikes anarchic freedom; he prefers to kick against the pricks, and react to an imposed given (though of course *bricoleurs,* too, or "tinkerers" as Jacob terms them, can also work only with what is to hand).

A further reason why Tournier leaves the consecrated Fall out of his variant story is that he wants to proceed instead in terms of character-types, contrasting modes of being, rather than significant, one-off events. In order to offset external causalism, or psychoanalysis, Tournier often turns to the rather old-fashioned pseudo-science of *caractérologie,* which can be adapted to suit his fondness for idiosyncrasy, perversity, and monstrosity. One particular set of standard pairs in *caractérologie* comprises *primaire/secondaire*.[5] Tournier asks us to forget the scholastic resonances, which are likely "de s'y attacher comme une mauvaise odeur" (*VV,* p. 232). In his use of the concepts, the *primaire* individual is uninhibitedly locked into a present perpetually reborn; the *secondaire* more introvertly into a past full of echoes. It is never clear whether Tournier emulates the binary polarities of Gide or Lévi-Strauss—two admitted mentors—or whether he *plays* between both. "Il ne faut pas céder à la tentation de valoriser l'une des catégories caractérologiques aux dépens de la catégorie opposée" (*VV,* p. 337).

After being expelled from Paradise, without explanation, Adam and Eve suffer long years of wandering in the desert. Or rather Adam is happy there and Eve miserable. Individual and habitat are virtually synonymous for Tournier, who frequently writes of his house, an ex–vicarage, as if it were some kind of living partner to himself. On their wanderings, Adam and Eve produce Cain and Abel, the latter stereotypically male and the former feminized. Cain drinks in Eve's entrancing tales about the lost Paradise. He is made for stay-at-home activities: gardening, farming, building. Meanwhile Abel, the spitting image of his father, wants only locomotion and contest. Brotherly rivalry very early turns them into "frères ennemis." Abel delights in wrecking Cain's juvenile constructions.

When Cain later starts building Eden 2 (no doubt a joky reference to all the satellite burghs of Paris), God grows angry with him, as he had earlier been with Adam, but for different reasons. Whereas Adam had disobediently not wanted to settle down and multiply, Cain is building or rebuilding what Adam and Eve had lost. Cain is in fact rivalling God by imposing order on chaos. In other versions of this myth, Cain is not normally the hero. In Hugo's poem "La Conscience," for example, after murdering his brother Cain tries ever more elaborate means of escape from God's judging eye, but even in a vault "l'oeil était toujours dans la tombe et regardait Caïn."[6] Tournier patently favors the underdog. Just as a stock theme of Westerns is the feud between cattlemen and farmers, so a vendetta festers between Abel and Cain. Betraying favoritism and thus showing himself not to be all-loving, God prefers the meat-offerings of Abel to the fruit and flowers of Cain. Eventually, after violent provocation, the pacifist, vegetarian Cain loses his temper and murders his carnivorous brother.

Now it is Cain's turn to be driven out, from his own Eden 2, and to spend many years wandering in the wilderness. Stubbornly, however, Cain returns to a spot close by the original paradise, and there builds the first city in history: Enoch, a marvellous, civilized place with, at its center, a majestic temple. He has overcome his damnation and come back to his preferred static existence, fortified by his experience of the opposite. This pattern reveals how the basic opposition of Cain and Abel can take different forms (as indeed it will in "L'Aire du Muguet"). As well as sharply defined antithesis, this myth can represent the coexistence, or the alternation, of the two tendencies within one person. Nomads cannot erect anything lasting: only tents, not temples. And sedentary people need the variant experience of travel, or as Thoreau said, "the tonic of wildness."[7]

God turns up. He has been brought down to earth, and is worn out by all his peregrinations with his favored sons of Abel. He has been jolted about on his long travels with the Ark of the Covenant across the deserts. He is in fact looking for a home in which to rest his weary bones. The grandson Cain welcomes the decrepit forbear. Instead of the prodigal son, "c'est le retour du père avare."[8] Grumpy God is solemnly installed in his waiting temple, which he will never again quit. Tournier's God is a clumsy, self-centered bungler: partial, not omniscient, nor even all-powerful. Just as Tournier enjoys making marginal people central, so here he revels in hijacking signs and turning the center of the Judeo-Christian tradition into a partly comic figure. The story has come full circle. At the start, original androgyny (God, Adam); at the finale a self-asserting hermaphrodite, a feminized male, Cain.

For Davis, this story "gives a concise version of the cycle of plenitude, loss and reconciliation which plays an important role in much of his writing."[9] Tournier here practices creative plagiarism, or adhocism, in tune with God's original copying. Thus Tournier induces both the sense of *déjà vu,* or *déjà lu,* and also he destabilizes such archetypes by extensions and twists.

Is there a moral to this fable, written in a mock-simple narrative style but loaded with ideas, as always with Tournier? Man, softened and feminized, teaches God a lesson and puts him in his place. The best place for God would appear to be in church, where he can do no, or less, mischief. And the best kind of human being is a harmonious admixture of the female and the male, the settler who has travelled.

2
Closure of the Myth: "La Fin de Robinson Crusoé"

From a wilderness Eden ("La Famille Adam"), or a walled garden ("Amandine"), or, here, to a desert island, Tournier rings changes on closed perfection. In its own small way, does this tale, the shortest in the collection after "La Mère Noël," seek to deconstruct or at least redirect *Vendredi ou les limbes du Pacifique*, Tournier's remake, umpteenth in the series, of the Crusoe story? In the novel, Tournier's version of Robinson refuses to leave his beloved island, Speranza, whereas Vendredi goes, lured by the glimpse of Western civilization offered by the rescue ship. In "La Fin de Robinson Crusoé," both master and formerly happy dancing partner have gone to England. The subject matter is thus a rewrite of *Vendredi;* and none of its material comes from Daniel Defoe's text.

Tournier's hindsight or "aft-boding" grants the younger Robinson prescience: "Si Robinson refuse de quitter Speranza, c'est parce qu'il pressent le terrible coup de vieux qu'il attraperait en réintégrant la société." (*VP*, p. 300)[1] As it turns out, in this followup tale, he will have to reseek the island in order to become fully and cruelly aware of this aging. This story is another slant on coming down to earth. God in "La Famille Adam" benefits from this translation; Robinson suffers bitterly.

The mythical hero has beached in a sleazy dockside pub, and is now an old drunk. The narrator is presumably one of the regulars; he mentions "notre table." (*FRC*, p. 22). Eighteen years after regressing to England with Vendredi and tales of twenty-two years of fantastic adventures on his island, Robinson has married. The entire missing chunk of his life overseas—the fullness rather than the hole—seems to have been decently buried. Yet his ordinary family life has started to come apart at the seams. Vendredi, seduced by European ways, has become a roaring tosspot, and has possibly begotten two bastards. Robinson has nonetheless stayed loyal to his old mate. Everyone wonders what binds them so tightly. Suspected of theft, Vendredi vanishes. On his own now, Robinson concludes that Vendredi has gone back to their island.

The island had been Robinson's youth and vigor, his paradise. Widowed, he sets off on a return voyage. Arriving back years later on an old cargo boat, he is in an even worse state of drunken decrepitude than when he set out. His island has proved unlocatable. An old helmsman present in the tavern surmises that Robinson did in fact find his island, but failed to recognize it. Old age has intervened, and has in effect blinded him.

The ending is bleakly melancholy; even the raucous laughter in the pub is silenced. For who could be amused at this reminder of lost youth, the drooping of imaginative intensity, as well as of bodily energy and stamina? The lesson is harsh: there is no going back. Robinson should have remembered his earlier oath: "Il n'allait pas s'arracher à cet éternel présent, posé en équilibre à la pointe d'un paroxysme de perfection, pour choir dans un monde d'usure, de poussière et de ruines!"(*VLP,* p. 246). "La Fin de Robinson Crusoé" is another of Tournier's variants on the theme of lost paradises. In "La Fugue du petit Poucet," the old are the villains. Here, they are the accursed.

3
Creation of Legend: "La Mère Noël"

This tale, first published in *Elle* as "Le Réveillon du Petit Jésus," is one of several "Christmas tales" in *Le Coq de bruyère*.[1] Its humor is wilfully provincial and traditional. The name of the village, Pouldreuzic, suggests a Breton locale, a setting which plausibly engenders polarities, opposite camps: the lay teacher and supporters versus the local priest and parishioners. As always, Tournier works into the opposition some interchange or mediation. The antithesis here is duplicated by that between the pagan figure of Father Christmas and the Christian emblem of the Christ child. From the former the local children receive presents, whereas the latter provides them with a charming and edifying spectacle. Christmastime, notoriously, is the season of goodwill to all men.

The first sly joke is the announcement in the village that midnight mass will, "for reasons of convenience," be celebrated at 6 p.m. It will feature, inevitably, a "living crèche" or tableau. At the same hour, the state schoolteacher, dressed as Santa Claus, will dole out toys to pupils. This ceremony, like the "heathen Christmas-tree," is regarded as diabolical by the more fervently Catholic locals. The storm in the coffee bowl is thus set in motion. The new teacher is a woman. Which camp will she support? As she is divorced, the anticlerical set claim her for their own. On the other hand, she has been seen attending church. She is patently a conciliator, for while she agrees to be Santa Claus like her predecessors, she lends her three-month-old baby for the living crèche, to act the part of baby Jesus. The chiasmus perennially fascinates Tournier as a rhetorical as well as an interpersonal form.

All goes smoothly for a while on Christmas Eve. A real ox and ass gaze down benevolently on the human infant sleeping in the manger. As the priest mounts the pulpit, the baby begins to cry lustily, and seems about to wreck the whole ritual. In a nicely-judged touch, Tournier has the young girl playing the Virgin Mary cuddle the baby, fruitlessly, against her flat bosom. A choirboy fetches the mother from school; she arrives in her Father Christmas outfit. Beards in all other Tournier fictions (e.g., "Tupik") are blatant symbols of virility, generally of a repugnant kind. Here, the beard is one side of a bipartite unity. She ("il") approaches the manger, "he" unbuttons "his" tunic and offers a swelling breast to a swiftly pacified "petit Jésus."

A local legend is instantly born. This lactating Father Christmas is another unisex figure, like Adam and God in "La Famille Adam." In *Des Clefs et des serrures,* Tournier confesses his reversed ogre fixation, the result of seeing a rice lorry in India:

> Etre le camion-citerne lui-même et, telle une énorme truie aux cent tétines généreuses, donner mon ventre en pâture aux petits Indiens affamés. Ainsi l'Ogre, sous le coup d'une inversion bénigne, au lieu de manger les enfants, se fait manger par eux. (CS, p. 36)

It appears that Tournier posed for the photo on the publicity band: a man playing a woman playing a man's role—even more than usual of a sexual melting pot.[2]

Mme. Oiselin, the teacher, combines the planturous Earth-Mother (breasts) and the biblical patriarch (beard). She enacts in her cross-dressing a courageous compromise, squatting simultaneously on both sides of the fence and, implicitly, proving to the petty fanatics in each camp how stupid they are. She has crossed the dividing line. Her name, obviously suggestive of *oiseau,* indicates that, like the bird in various religious and mythological traditions, she is a link between heaven and earth, and a messenger of peace. Androgyne is superior to single-sex. Mme. Oiselin is truly an "alma mater." In "La Fugue du petit Poucet," we will see a male version: an "almus pater." In "La Mère Noël," a minor miracle has occurred, an everyday marvel. In his *contes,* Tournier makes up for the generally secondary placing of women and girls in his longer fictions. Mme. Oiselin, Amandine, Mélanie, Véronique, and the Baronne are all central foci in their respective tales.

4
The Good Initiation: "Amandine ou les deux jardins"

THE first three stories ("La Famille Adam," "La Fin de Robinson Crusoé" and "La Mère Noël") are largely gentle; even Robinson's impotent anguish wins respect from his onlookers. They are all straightforward in narrative line. The complications, and ambiguities, start with "Amandine ou les deux jardins." This is "un conte initiatique." For Tournier, children are essentially initiates, eagerly waiting to be let in on what life has in store for them; initiation and growing up are synonymous.[1] Binary patterns are once more at stake: child/adolescent, child/grown-up, female/male, human/animal, wild/tamed, good/bad, happiness/sorrow. Between these opposing categories Tournier introduces interchange and overlap. Amandine clambers over dividing walls.

Going on eleven years old, Amandine is not yet at "l'âge ingrat" or, as English puts it perhaps slightly more charitably, "the awkward age." According to Tournier, Rousseau is the great exponent of the belief that the prepubertal child—the properly educated one at least—is perfection. Tournier quotes Emile at twelve, "tout entier à son être actuel, et jouissant d'une plénitude de vie qui semble vouloir s'étendre hors de lui." (VV, p. 181)[2] Whereas round this age the child, of either sex, is for Tournier a (temporary) absolute, Rousseau sees this as only a staging post on the way to adulthood.

As it is a child's account of an adventure, Tournier keeps the style relatively simple, but the narrative shows, like many children themselves, an awareness beyond its impersonated years. The narrator Amandine sounds delectable: "Des yeux bleus, des lèvres vermeilles, des grosses joues roses, des cheveux blonds ondulés" (A, p. 35) She exhibits an unaffected narcissism; she is curious

4: THE GOOD INITIATION: "AMANDINE OU LES DEUX JARDINS"

about herself, but also about everything beyond herself. From the start, vacillations about gender occur. Her cat Claude bears a unisex name. When the ostensibly male cat gives birth to kittens, such doubts do not disappear, for the one retained kitten is given the sexually ambivalent name of Kamicha. Amandine observes with plausible childlikeness that the white spot over Kamicha's left eye is not the mark of an injury but more like the smear of a kiss from a flour-encrusted baker. Not "un oeil au beurre noir," then, but "au beurre blanc" (p. 36). Amandine is not only receptive but also observantly creative.

The narrative next moves from animals to humans, a recurrent pattern throughout the story. Amandine's comfortable bourgeois home is the scene of an absolutely orthodox division of labor. The house is mother's territory, and the garden father's. Both house and garden are always scrupulously neat. In "La Famille Adam," orderliness had been a human means of competing with God. Here it implies only boring predictability and safety, though Amandine does recognize the value of these unexciting qualities. She reports, deadpan, that everyone has to wear felt slippers in the house, and that there are ashtrays, even in the garden. Amandine appears largely sensible, non-extreme, not a goody-goody, but simply a good child. She likes the regularity of home and garden, but also finds it "un peu ennuyeux." (p. 36)

A small mystery arouses her interest. Where does Claude keep taking Kamicha? She must be initiating her kitten into something. Domestic cats are stereotypically the most enigmatic of creatures; and Tournier has written entertainingly of his own cat Sacha's disappearing acts (VI, p. 17). Cats are wandering home-birds, like Cain. Amandine notes perceptively how mistrustful cats are of food offered to them, dropping and sniffing it before devouring or scorning. She eventually deduces that the secretive Claude leads Kamicha over the wall into a neighboring garden. After a period of three months, Amandine senses that the kitten is now almost feral.

For the first time, Amandine speaks of her moments free of parental surveillance. These are when she rises early, before them, and watches the animal life of the garden. It is a time of overlap and coexistence, when the night animals and the day ones share the same space (unlike the brutal warfare of daytime gulls and nocturnal rats in *Les Météores*). In "Amandine," Tournier makes no room for the topos of Nature as "red in tooth and claw." To Amandine's eyes, the varied animals seem to have sorted themselves out amicably. Throughout the story, animals are ahead of humans. Nature is the most reliable pedagogue.

Though cats are traditionally credited with nine lives, Claude and Kamicha settle for two, one each side of the party wall. When Kamicha regresses one day and restarts to suck its mother, who is herself lapping milk from a saucer, Amandine imagines, in her state of still charming ignorance, that there is an unbroken channel: milk in at the mouth, warmed inside, and out at the teat. Then she sees Claude cuff Kamicha in order to remind it that it is a big boy/girl now and beyond the suckling stage. Inspired by the daring expeditions of the cats, Amandine decides to explore over the wall. Like Robinson's island or the Eden of "La Famille Adam" gardens are enclosed spaces; "Paradise" means "a walled garden." Amandine intuits that her parents would disapprove of such trespassing. They might, we are invited to speculate, decide that she is growing up too quickly. It is significant that they take no part in initiating her into any of the mysteries (gender, motherhood) that are intriguing her. All her diary entries are on Wednesdays and Sundays, when there is no school. She goes to the garden for a true education, like Tupik in the maze of the little park.

From this point on, all of her emotions are mixed. She is at a pivotal, transitional age. When she clambers into the next-door garden with some difficulty, she finds it overgrown, seemingly dangerous and troubling, but her curiosity makes her persist with this journey into the unknown. This section reveals Tournier, a great admirer of Colette and of Giono, at his most pagan and pantheistic. Like those masters, he animates all he touches, flora or fauna. Kamicha, a kind of animal double, acts as a pathfinder through the dense wilderness. It leads Amandine to a statuette of a young boy with wings: Cupid/Eros. Significantly, he has dropped his symbolic armaments: bow, arrows and quiver. His face looks sad to Amandine, and he is androgynous in appearance. Humanity has introduced love, and therefore trouble and strife, into the previously self-sufficient wild garden. The joys of sex, clearly (or mistily), have their melancholy side; and the secret of puberty is bittersweet. Semi-lost in this suburban jungle, Amandine feels a long way from her secure home and its tidy garden, and she wonders whether she will ever get back. That is, ever be the same as

4: THE GOOD INITIATION: "AMANDINE OU LES DEUX JARDINS"

before her initiation. In case this sounds like a total break, a before-and-after, we should remember how Claude suckled Kamicha when the kitten was already too old for it. Children do not leave one stage for another; they shuttle.

After a short sleep back in the familiar haven of her own bed, nothing seems to have altered, except for a trace of blood on her leg, menstrual blood, which she, like many uninformed girls before her, thinks of as a wound. Gazing in the mirror, as at the start of the story, she decides that she looks rather like the boy statuette. Something has in fact changed, in the direction of complication. The unisex Kamicha reappears, swollen-bellied. The same destiny is presumably potential for Amandine. Via the cat, she is on the verge of discovering a vocation: fecundity. In case this appears mindlessly sexist, it should be recalled that the earlier description of day and night animals stressed overlap and coexistence. The sexes, too, are closer than conventional demarcations allow. The feminized Eros suggests a defeat or surrender of virility, for he has laid down his arms. The cat whose tail stuck up straight like an erection has turned out female. At the end, then, Amandine feels in-between: between childhood and adolescence, between female and male. She has two gardens, unlike her compartmentalized father. She is starting to acquire the confidence associated with males, while retaining the promise of riches like a female. (Tournier is even-handed, as interested in virilized women—cf. his projected novel on ex-East German athletes—as in feminized men). The very contiguity of the two contrasting gardens, and the possibility of *enjambement*, as attractive to venturesome children as to poets, adds to the mix.

"Faire le mur," which is what Amandine has achieved, signifies also convicts going over the top, jail-breaking. She is just beginning to escape from the prison-house of ignorance and inexperience. Tournier never implies that childhood is a state of empty innocence, and is indeed strongly suspicious of the very concept of purity. Those who want to keep children's literature pure-minded seek, in his view, to deprive children of reality, to stunt their emotional and intellectual growth, and thus to reduce their humanity. Such censorship lies behind the fear of children "finding out too soon." Taking risks so often, Tournier has recently lifted his young heroine even further out of nescience towards dizzy heights:

> Qu'est-ce que la métaphysique? "Méta," ça veut dire de l'autre côté et "physique," c'est le mur. Le métaphysicien est celui qui saute le mur pour voir de l'autre côté du mur ce qui s'y passe. Amandine, c'est la métaphysique, c'est Platon, c'est Aristote, c'est Plotin, c'est Saint Thomas. Ils sont allés voir de l'autre côté du mur, ils ont vu des choses bouleversantes. Ils reviennent ensuite chez les hommes mais ils savent, et plus rien ne sera comme avant.[3]

There is a follow-up to the story. In an interview in *Le Monde* in 1977, when this text first appeared in an illustrated children's book, Tournier shows how even his smaller fictions widen out to larger issues.[4] Firstly, he queries the stock idea that country children (but Amandine is bourgeoise, not a peasant lass) learn about the "facts of life" from observing animals. He claims to know many youngsters fully conversant with animal reproduction but who fail to see the connection with human sexuality. He makes his usual sharp distinction between initiation (a gentle learning process under sympathetic guidance) and mere information, which he believes has ruled Western school curricula since the eighteenth century. Some adult readers jibbed at the mention of menstruation in a children's story. Tournier counters: most initiation rites, (also known as "puberty rites"), involve blood. He is thinking of ritual circumcision and body-scarring in some tribal societies. He has of course to acknowledge that such societies more often conduct initiation rites for boys than for girls. In Central Africa, for instance, boys are encouraged to "die to" their mothers so as to integrate themselves into a male adult society. Typically, Tournier sees this crossover more as a crisscross, for the men become the new "mothers" of the boys.

The vestige of such practices in western society is the repellent hazing that goes on in some schools and armies. Tournier also mentions brutal surgical interventions, such as the traumatic tonsillectomy he underwent himself as a child.[5] To all this he adds mischievously school examinations, that great "bourgeois initiation-rite." Yet none of this, to him, adds up to real initiatory benefits. The notorious permissiveness of our society is in fact repressive, as Marcuse was arguing in the 1960s. More urgently relevant today is youth unemployment. The growing militant protest against this particularly alienating form of exclusion from the adult world is an increasingly serious social problem.

Girls, he maintains, have a different fate. They are more cen-

4: THE GOOD INITIATION: "AMANDINE OU LES DEUX JARDINS"

trally and continuously integrated into society (i.e., into conformity) by the way they are brought up, close to mothers and taught to emulate them. There is, he admits, a girl's form of initiation, but it is centrifugal, breaking away from the orthodox centre, instead of being admitted to it, like boys by older men. Where can a girl go, except into open revolt? This is in his view the dilemma of Women's Liberation: the only option is permanent flight.

In the story, Amandine comes home again, somewhat wiser, but there is no hint that she will break out of her female destiny or flee her family. While Tournier, in both interview and story, is patently sympathetic to women, his standards remain those of a male. He prefers to see women as more stable, more fruitful, than men. That is, for him, woman's glory. Not a few women might think that such glory is more like a millstone round the neck.

As the cats Claude and Kamicha with Amandine, Tournier leads readers up the garden path. The collection increases in complexity, and kinkiness, after a mildish opening set of stories. Tournier is initiating his readers, of whatever age, breaking them in gently. As Proust said, "il est vain d'écrire spécialement pour les enfants. Ce qui féconde un enfant, ce n'est pas un livre d'enfantillages."[6]

5
Child Father to Man: "La Fugue du petit Poucet"

THIS is another Christmas story which promises a happy ending. It recycles the famous children's story of Tom Thumb, le petit Poucet, collected and retold by Charles Perrault in the seventeenth century, though it was current in England in the sixteenth.[1] In Perrault's version, poverty-stricken parents try to abandon their seven sons in the forest. They end up in the Ogre's house where, through Tom's ingenuity, the Ogre's seven daughters are slaughtered in their stead. By stealing the Ogre's seven-league boots, the boys, Poucet in the lead again, swindle the Ogress out of all the couple's gold. It is a tale of superior mother-wit centered on the resourcefulness of the puniest child of the family. Tournier works several twists on the standard inversion of little beating big. He leaves out the pebbles incident, as his minuscule hero has no wish to find his way home but rather to vacate it; and he is an only child. Tournier sets the traditional tale in the present to give contemporary point to the old story.

Petit Poucet and his mother are faced, without option, with a change of abode from suburbs to city, from ground level to the twenty-third floor of a tower block. The father is an ogre in the everyday sense, a man ruled by tyrannical *idées fixes*. His job as a tree surgeon suggests that bogyman of psychoanalysis: the castrating genitor. The tree is also an age-old symbol for the human frame. To the mother's queries as to how she can shake her carpets from that altitude, he replies that there is no need, as the windows are hermetically sealed. The family will be, in effect, insulated against reality, not even hearing the jets roaring past every forty-five seconds: "comme dans un sous-marin" (*FPP*, p. 50). Poucet senior condemns himself, and the modern demands

5: CHILD FATHER TO MAN: "LA FUGUE DU PETIT POUCET"

he espouses, out of his own mouth, backed up by the president of France himself: "'Il faut que Paris s'adapte à l'automobile, un certain esthétisme dût-il en souffrir'." (p. 51)

When le petit Poucet asks the naive but telling question: Why? the reply is that the government's plans for a new Paris geared to cars entail chopping down all its trees to make room for expressways. When the boy further asks about the boots promised him for Christmas, the father offers a color television instead. Prefabricated magic is the best he can manage. His son decides to run away—the *fugue* of the title.[2] Fugues in music also involve the upending of themes. Both Poucet and Amandine need to escape their families in order to have formative experiences. Poucet's farewell note houses malapropisms that capture his semi-awareness (a mishearing is a near miss) of what awaits him if he stays. "Je ne veux pas d'éclairage au néant, ni d'air contingenté" (p. 52). Unaware of his inklings, Pierre worries about his spelling. His word hoard is jumbled, but his instincts play him true.

He heads for the forest, the site of so many traditional tales, in the hope of finding gypsies who will take him in. In a variant of Tournier's leitmotif of *la phorie,* Poucet is borne away by a kindly lorry driver. High up in the cab, the child imagines he is riding an elephant. Imaginatively again, he transforms the lorry's lights and decorations into a Christmas tree. Another quest gets under way. Dropped off, he loses himself in the forest and settles down to sleep, using as a living quilt the three pet rabbits he has brought with him to save them from an unrabbitlike life on the twenty-third story. It is a fair exchange; he feels he is the rabbits' warren. Lights and laughing voices wake him up. Seven little girls, the magic number, imprison him, to his great delight.

Their forest home is in total contrast with the hated tower-block. It is old, lived-in, cozy, open-plan. Logs burn in the grate; a forgivable exploitation of trees by man. The slogan on the wall, "Faites l'amour, ne faites pas la guerre," dating from anti–Vietnam war protests, prepares the ground for the girls' father, a hippy. Sex roles have been switched. The mother is on the road, selling her fabrics, while father Logre keeps house. "Un vrai géant des bois," he is gentle, has long blond hair held by a shoelace across his brow, a golden beard and magnificent, heavily embroidered boots. Pierre is bowled over and can manage only: "Vous êtes beau comme une femme," a nice counterweight to Adam's male chauvinism in "La Famille Adam" (p. 57). The family keep dissolving in infectious laughter which, here, has the complexity of simplicity, not of ambivalence, as in "Que ma joie demeure." The boy has a wonder-filled Christmas with his newfound family.

The food is vegetarian, whereas ogres are stereotypically flesh-eating. Logre sings to a guitar in a high-pitched voice. He is the *almus pater*, the pendant to la Mère Noël. Passing joints around to the children, he talks about trees as the most important things in the world. Paradise, he teaches, was a forest, whose every tree belonged to a different species, most of them now extinct. The top tree was the Tree of Knowledge (lopped from the Eden of "La Famille Adam"), although all possessed some magic property. A greedy, jealous God forbade Adam to eat of the Tree of Knowledge, on pain of death. Calling the divine obscurantist bluff, Adam survived, but his disobedience alarmed his maker, who sensed a future rival. And so God placed angels with flaming swords at the gateway of Paradise; he exiled Adam and Eve to the treeless desert, the realm of hunting and violence. Trees, for their part, represent tranquil growth, and form a bridge between supposed contraries: high and low, sky and earth (as many ancient mythologies propose). Trees are equilibrium and health. They offer a model: not so much the Tree of Knowledge as the tree *as* knowledge, embodied wisdom.[3] Logre is preaching a secular, Green sermon, an ecological lesson. The imagination needs a solid foundation, just as the upreaching trunk needs roots. A home in midair is no home at all. Trees are also dependent on wind, which supplies the breath of life to leaves. Trees are thus interconnected with the whole of nature: wind, water, soil, sky. If traffic asphyxiates the arteries of the modern city, a different traffic (exchange, interchange) animates the natural world. Though secular, Logre's sermon also echoes biblical themes such as the Holy Spirit, often pictured in terms of wind or breath. (See *Les Météores* and *Le Vent Paraclet*). Possibly nervous of seeming to preach even politically correct ideology, Tournier mitigates the pedagogical ponderousness by suggesting that Logre's speech is all induced, or at least released, by marijuana. For his part, petit Poucet now thinks he sees a tree floating in the air of the cottage. The children all flop into a communal bed. In Tournier's fiction, such promiscuity is unfailingly delectable. Pierre revels in an orgy of delight: tickles, caresses, fun, laughter. "On sait que les contes de fées sont les romans érotiques des enfants."[4]

At dawn they are all forced back to gray reality, when police begin hammering, with the sound of axes hacking trees, on the cottage door. Logre appears in modified hippy dress, more like Jesus Christ in familiar pictures (but recall the Jesus freaks): long robe, barefooted. His calm remark: "Les soldats de Yahvé viennent m'arrêter" (p. 63) suggests that the Son of God is being punished by an avenging father.[5] The police in fact accompany the vengeful Poucet senior, the Holy Father's coarse vicar on earth. Before being led off, Logre offers petit Poucet a gift. The boy rejects jewels and plumps for the wondrous boots, which are leaning over like an elephant's ears. These will be the vehicles of dream travel. Takeoff is possible only from a solid grounding.

"A l'ogre qui fait peur aux enfants fait place l'ogre qui fait peur aux adultes."[6] Retarded grown-ups. According to the forces of law and order, Logre's crimes are: drug-taking, abduction of a minor, and (the pacifist slogan) attempting to demoralize the army. Pierre's father loathes the forest and its proud stands of trees. In Paris, too, he complains, the Bois de Boulogne is "un lupanar à ciel ouvert" (p. 64). Chopping down trees and excising sexual pleasure are all one to him.

The story ends with Pierre's parents watching Yuletide festivities on television. Alone in his room, their son tries on the outsize boots. "Ce sont des bottes de rêve" in two senses: firstly, the advertising cliché, and secondly, literally, dream-boots. They set him free to wander in his imagination while his body lies on the bed. He dreams that he is a tree, and that he is therefore in touch with every particle of the universe. He chooses trees against his axe-wielding father. Petit Poucet is "immensément heureux" (p. 65). He is *le vagabond immobile* that Tournier exults in being, when not travelling spatially. If the text preaches, its little hero does not, for he makes no effort to convert his probably too far gone father. Like Amandine, he contains something of both sexes. Both are *enfants sages*. Whereas Amandine is on the verge of puberty, Pierre seems still in a state of neotony, arrested sexual development (see VV, pp. 194–95). He is a divine child, great in intuitive wisdom, if pint-size. Far gentler than his father, he has female values: peace, dreaming, natural growth, warmth, sharing.

Tournier has frequently admitted his fascination with children, mainly between the ages of eight and fourteen, presumably because they would progressively come to disappoint him as they grew out of childhood. He has had no children of his own, and indeed would seem to prefer that human beings were engendered by virgin birth. Tournier's religion is indeed Peter Pantheism, as is indicated by his envy of stasis (cf. his gloss on Boubat's photograph of a hen beneath a tree: "L'arbre et la poule sont figés dans la conscience du rôle fondamental qui leur incombe: incarner des symboles de permanence, de fidélité, de confiance. Boubat ou la douceur de l'être") (CS, p. 71). Tournier has regularly borrowed children from consenting and entirely trusting friends to live with him for long periods.

In "La Fugue du petit Poucet" the child is father to the man, who betrays him. A further moral of this story is that fairy tales did not happen only in some legendary past. They can be alive and well and living in a tower-block. Poucet might be the child wilfully starved of fairy stories by his anti–imaginative father that Bruno Bettelheim pities.[7] Fantasy is desperately needed, not as a luxury, but as a vitally constituent part of authentic development, and as a counterbalance to the prosaic reality we must inhabit most of the time.

Because he is a young child, Poucet's lack of inches is not stressed by Tournier, whose interest in dwarfs will get a full outing in "Le Nain rouge": the belligerent midget, the pocket marauder, after the peace-loving Poucet.

6
Sex and Confusion: "Tupik"

THE young hero, or rather agonist, of this tale is a poignant creature who, lacking initiation and indeed badly let down by grown-ups, commits a tragic error. We see him first flinching from a kiss thrust at him by an insensitive father—a rebarbative man whose repellent facial hair has earned Tupik his nickname ("Tu piques!"). The boy does not want to be what he has been nominated, just as we will gradually find out that he refuses the gender assigned to him.

In contrast with the prickly father, Tupik's mother is all soft and feminine, perfumed and powdered. She soothes her child's irritation, at least on an epidermic level. When she tells him that baby hedgehogs do not prick, but only adult males, Tupik is launched on the path of renouncing future manhood. The boy has watched his father shaving with a cut-throat razor, but has never witnessed his mother dressing, hence his obsession with the mystery of women's toilet (and later with ladies' toilets). Her lack of true warmth is revealed when, all dolled up to go out, she keeps him at a distance from her made-up face behind its veil. The crisscross is here frustrating: Tupik is offered the unwanted paternal kiss, and denied the maternal. He has to make do with a substitute, the first stage of a fetish: her glove.

The very bourgeois house they inhabit has in its corridor a heavily symbolic Pre-Raphaelite painting, a Judgment Day, where humanity is sorted out into the damned and the elect. Tupik notices that the damned are the dark, hairy males, and the saved delicate, pale females. Art thus corroborates his direct experience.

The scene switches to a quiet little square with its public gardens, where nannies take their middle class charges to play in the afternoon after morning school (to Tupik a kind of prison, resolutely removed from the real world). In contrast, the square is a magic site of initiation, like the second garden in "Amandine." It boasts classical statues, one of a centaur, a hybrid (half man, half horse) carrying off a halfheartedly struggling maiden. When Tupik asks his nanny, Marie, what is going on, he receives a garbled answer (cf. petit Poucet's malapropisms, also the result of mishearing and misapprehension). Marie has taken "centaure" for "sent-fort." Recalling the pungent toiletries of his father, Tupik feels disgusted. A further mythological statue represents Theseus killing the Minotaur (another hybrid: half human, half bull). Theseus, however, is wearing the short Greek kilt and, it seems to Tupik, has a girl's name (Thésée). He is extremely confused. All the adults in this tale talk and behave more evasively, illogically, childishly than Tupik himself, who maintains a grave, focused, if largely bewildered gaze.

The regular attendants of the square include old Cromorne, who wears a uniform and is twice mutilated in that he lost an arm in the war and his wife later.[1] With childlike logic, Tupik wonders whether there is a connection between the two losses. In a phrase which anticipates the shocking climax to the story, Tupik imagines that Cromorne severed his left arm at his wife's funeral in order to place it in offering on her coffin. The other regulars, Parisian stereotypes or Proustian reminiscences, are Mlle. Aglaé, who has the chair concession, and Mme. Béline, who runs a confectionery stall. The entire mini-society of the square survives on congealed rituals.

What interests Tupik above all are the public conveniences, divided of course (as on Judgment Day) into Gents and Ladies. The attendant is Mamouse, who guards the entrance like the hound Cerberus in Hades. On her table are a saucer for the coins left by relieved visitors, and a little primus stove for heating up her meal, invariably a stew of poultry innards. The whole adult world of the square is obsessed by minutiae, whereas Tupik ponders, stumblingly, the huge questions of life, death, and sex. Mamouse is something of an ogress. Tupik overhears her ponderous joke about the cacophonous noises made by men in public toilets, and her tirades about how disgusting men in general are: more grist to the boy's busily whirring mill.

Tupik's problem is how to evade this guardian's eagle eye and slip into the Ladies, which fascinates him as forbidden territory for a male. As it happens, he has got into the habit of urinating not upright but squatting. Once in the street he had aped a dog peeing on a lamppost by cocking his leg likewise. His unamused mother slapped him, and he concluded that anything to do with micturition is a source of unpleasantness. When, quite expectably, he starts to wet his bed as a result of his mini-trauma, his nanny, in the best tradition of adult sensitivity, threatens him with the surgical removal of his "robinet." This might have been the end of the story but, as it is by Tournier, "les choses s'enchaînèrent de la façon la plus diabolique" (*T*, p. 79).

The angelic agent of this diabolic turn is Tupik's friend, Dominique, whom Tupik spots emerging from the Ladies. Dominique's father owns the carousel on which Tupik always chooses the little locomotive, where he feels safe in the enclosed space. Dominique is a big, motherly boy, calm and protective. When Tupik asks him why he uses the Ladies, Dominique promises him the answer—the first truthful one Tupik will receive—half an hour later, at the heart of the little maze (cf. the reference to Theseus earlier, who found the monster Minotaur in the center of a labyrinth). This maze is an enclosed space within the larger fenced public garden. Tupik picks his way through the dense, mossy foliage. At the core he finds a pedestal lacking a statue (contrast "Amandine"). Instead, Dominique is squatting on top of the vacated plinth. After a few children's ritual gestures (swearing, and spitting on the ground), Dominique unbuttons to reveal that he is a girl (his father dresses him as a boy for the sake of the machine-minding side of the business). He tells Tupik: "Tu comprendras ça plus tard," which is what children are forever being fobbed off with by adults, but it is meant literally here (p. 82). A double absence at the heart of the maze, then: no statue on the pedestal, no penis on the supposed boy Dominique.

Tupik frets over these conundrums and works out his own solution. He has caught sight of a grown man urinating, and been appalled by the spectacle of his naked organ—hideous and superfluous, in Tupik's eyes. He instantly makes a link (he is a puerile poet, forever making comparisons and seeking to combine disparate fragments), a diabolical link, with the bits of meat simmering in Mamouse's casserole. He thinks he now understands the statue of Theseus and the Minotaur. What the hero was attacking with his sword was the beast's genitals. Thus all the threads of the story are pulled together, logically or insanely. Tupik stops wetting his bed. Marie calls off her threat to summon a surgeon to chop off his offending "tap." Armed with his father's cut-throat razor, Tupik advances on Mamouse and amputates before her amazed gaze his small penis, which he then offers, as if in sacrifice, to the goddess of the locale, presumably so that she add it to her ever-bubbling, chicken-pieces stew. Not surprisingly, Tupik then faints.

Tournier is prone to disclaim responsibility for his more outrageous incidents. In answer to the question as to who impaled the three children at the climax of *Le Roi des aulnes*, he said: "Qui? Mais tout le roman, bien sûr, la poussée irrésistible d'une masse de petits faits et notations accumulées" (*VP*, p. 126). This is plot as infernal machine, and fictional ending as final solution. Another novelist, speaking no doubt for most of his colleagues, once said in reply to a question as to how he viewed fiction: "You just take reality and water it down." It is statistically likely that some boy, somewhere, has amputated himself for Tupik's reasons: disgust of being male, envy of being female. If Tupik had been older, he might have settled for a sex-change operation. When Tupik sees Dominique's female genitals, he does not register them as a lack, as in Freudian theory, which credits some young girls with penis envy. Tupik feels penis revulsion. Not a lack, but an excess. Even-handedly, Bruno Bettelheim concludes from his clinical experience: "It seems that desire for the opposite sex's characteristics and potentialities is common to both men and women."[2] Tupik is exceptional, but not unbelievable.

It is a tragic little tale. The only solution Tupik can think up for his dilemma is a diminution, a mutilation, and a bad mistake. Merely amputating a male does not create a female. Yet there remains a perverse logic in his act. His father had put him off ever wanting to grow up as an orthodox male.

Tupik's view of the division of the sexes, centered on public lavatories, has therefore to do with evacuation of waste matter and not with erotic pleasure. Given his age, this is understandable. Besides, Tournier himself is as fascinated by scatology as by sexuality. He thought of assuming as pseudonym for his first novel his great-grandmother's name, Anus.[3] Tupik does not get the best of both worlds, like Amandine or petit Poucet. He is the victim of a segregated world. Neither "pure" woman nor "pure" man comes off well in this story. Only Dominique seems at ease in her/his skin and unisex name. Via Tupik, Tournier appeals to the child buried (alive) in the adult. He is an insolent writer, and nobody is more insolent (etymologically: unaccustomed, fresh-eyed, as well as arrogant) than a questioning child.

Gardens are, for Tournier, places of initiation; here for the worse, in "Amandine" for the probably better. In a recent text, Tournier links childhood with adult cruelty, "l'affinité qui rapproche jardin d'enfants et jardin des supplices."[4] It could be that Tupik's self-mutilation is a displacement of the horrific, gory tonsillectomy performed on the conscious Tournier as a child (see VP, pp. 17–18). Or a phantom temptation for the adult Tournier, who has protested so often the emphasis on genital sex. What is clear is that this story reflects Tournier's conviction that "l'enfance nous est donnée comme un chaos brûlant, et nous n'avons pas trop de tout le reste de notre vie pour tenter de le mettre en ordre et de nous l'expliquer" (VP, p. 19).

7
The Optative Mode: "Que ma joie demeure"

This is one of the four stories (the others: "Tristan Vox," "Les Suaires de Véronique," "Le Nain rouge,") concerned with fame, success, and their ambivalences. Another Christmas tale, it retains some religious overhang.

Names are identifying tags but loaded with potential extra meaning. We feel this instinctively, indeed superstitiously. Names often strike us as peculiarly appropriate, or splendidly unsuitable (Cardinal Sin of the Philippines); or just funny in themselves. People can not only rejoice in the name of X, but also squirm under the name of Y. Members of all societies, throughout recorded time, have played around with, read into, chewed over, names so much that the whole process deserves the coinage "onomastication." In heraldry, signifying names are called "talking" or "singing" names. In all these ways, names move way beyond mere labels. A belief, adhered to by Tournier, that names bear deeper significance is part of a wider faith in a totally meaning-full universe. For such minds, there is nothing solely functional or accidental about a person's name, or indeed anything else.

"Que ma joie demeure" emphasises from the outset the bizarre name of its hero: Raphaël Bidoche. The forename alludes to the archangel and the famous painter. At the other extreme, the surname evokes low-grade meat, scrag-end. The total name is thus an oxymoron, a favorite device of Tournier, who rejoices in forcing apparently very separate concepts to cohabit in a new partnership: an economical way of suggesting an inner split, tension, or alternation.

In his childhood years, all seems at first to go marvellously well for Raphaël Bidoche. He plays the piano like an angel (or an archangel), and is in addition a beautiful child. An infant prodigy. A prodigy is a variation on the theme of the monster, and is similarly

7: THE OPTATIVE MODE: "QUE MA JOIE DEMEURE"

singled out, set apart from the common run of mortals. Raphaël, then, starts off at the top. He will then fall from grace. And he will rise again.

The opening pages pastiche a certain kind of corny lyricism, pseudoartistic cliché. Hostesses fight over Raphaël for their *soirées musicales*. His prodigious talents give "high hopes" to his parents (again, as in other stories, largely conspicuous by their absence). Tournier is mocking the social chitchat and hype about genius. In the middle of this satirical takeoff, Tournier drops the name of Bach's superb chorale: "Joy of Man's Desiring." Whatever is laughable in Raphaël or those around him contains also this sublime potentiality: the interpretation and the performance of art at its highest level. Genius exists, even if we talk about it foolishly.

Giddy heights have to be supported by sheer hard work: years of practice, the daily grind. The "monster" Raphaël is sufficiently "normal" to envy other children who can play in the street while he practices indoors. Being special brings sadness and solitude. To complete the downward curve, puberty arrives (*la mauvaise fée*) to transmogrify the beautiful child into a gauche adolescent: bony, angular, shortsighted. "L'enfant épanoui est voué fatalement à une décrépitude qui s'appelle la puberté. Mauvaise fée, la puberté transforme en citrouille le carrosse qu'elle touche de sa baguette. L'équilibre moral se brise, la grâce physique s'enfuit" (*VV*, p. 182). Amandine is the prepubertal child, not yet struck by the disaster of adolescence, the stage which shifts the emphasis in Raphaël to the *bidoche* side.

He has clearly never experienced a true childhood; that was sacrificed on the altar of art. He thinks he has found a true partner in Bénédicte. The same clichéic style as earlier celebrates their seemingly idyllic love. "Ils vivaient d'amour, de musique et d'eau claire" (*QMJD*, p. 89): they made beautiful music together. "Joy of Man's Desiring" becomes their theme song, "our tune." Even so, when Raphaël plays this piece, it sounds like the sublime, cosmic laughter of God himself: pure joy (ibid.).

The serpent in this mini-Eden is the need to earn money in order to set up house. When Raphaël is offered a job in a night club playing cheapjack music, it is Bénédicte (bless her) who supplies the clinching arguments against his instinctive reluctance to prostitute his talent. Raphaël is paid to accompany a fourth-rate *chansonnier* called Bodruche (spelled *baudruche*, it means windbag). Bodruche's act milks jokes about misfortune: a whole chain of fiascos, an escalation of mediocrity. The laughter that greets this performance is anything but godlike. It is cynical, sadistic, corrupted and corrupting. Bodruche drags his audience down to his level; he does not uplift them. The laughter he generates is negative, diabolical. It is this fallen creature that Raphaël has to accompany, and inevitably, by the contagion of baseness, he starts to get sucked down. Even their names, Bidoche and Bodruche, rhyme with each other, roughly.

Everything seems to be conspiring against Raphaël: his fiancée Bénédicte, his employer, his partner Bodruche. The young pair's idyll is changing into the archetypal modern marriage, obsessed with bills to pay and material acquisitions. Money is the god and the millstone. The degradation of the cherub prodigy increases when he is tempted to do a solo performance at the club. The act preceding his is grotesque—a tango executed by a gigantic woman and a dwarf. And so, when Raphaël comes on stage, wearing glasses and a stiff suit, the audience coarsely imagines that his will be another comedy routine and greets him with derisive laughter. When he then has problems with his piano stool and wrecks it, and when he drops his glasses and has to crawl round myopically searching for them, the audience goes wild. He has given them pure farce, knockabout comedy. He has triumphed, accidentally and wrongly. This is what his big chance, the solo performance he has been working and waiting for, has turned into. The prodigy has become a freak, a clown.

Raphaël and Bénédicte are now comfortably off. One day, an old friend, a violinist who has not sold out for a fast franc, visits them. This visit jolts Raphaël's conscience, but not enough to lift him off the rails set down for him. Logically, he ends up performing his eccentric number in a circus, at Christmastime. Bénédicte acts as his stooge, the white-faced clown, whereas Raphaël plays the red clown, "l'Auguste," the clumsy failure. All his props are a source of comic surprise. His clothes, his piano stool and the instrument itself conceal jets of water, rude noises: farts and burps. It is a diabolic piano. The circus audience rocks with laughter. His sole saving grace is his myopia; he can see only an anonymous seething mass in their misty seats.

Then something extraordinary happens. Tournier introduces as a question the possibility of a miracle. The climax of Raphaël's

7: THE OPTATIVE MODE: "QUE MA JOIE DEMEURE"

act is supposed to be the controlled explosion of his "diabolical" piano, releasing sausages, cream cakes, hams, etc. Instead, Raphaël sits quietly down at the keyboard, the uproar subsides, and he begins to play "Que ma joie demeure." The instrument itself, a clapped-out circus joanna, seems to be transformed under his magical touch. Once again, as in the past, divine laughter breaks forth and replaces satanic sniggering.

As Worton puts it, "each of [Tournier's] novels ends in a moment of sublimation and transmogrification—as do most of his short stories."[1] Raphaël's apotheosis here is to re-become, at least temporarily, the child prodigy he was before. But the message is more mixed than that. Tournier's work, and tone, swing, like Raphaël's career, between the ridiculous and the sublime. "Que ma joie demeure" proclaims that art, good and great art, will out. Yet what Raphaël Bidoche has achieved is maybe just a reprieve, a one-off. It may be his swan song. Note the optative mood of the title: let my joy be lasting. Raphaël's guardian angel has released him, possibly only on parole, from his Bidoche side. His name contains the high and the low. At the end, the high triumphs over the low. But can anyone live continuously at such altitude?

8
Purifying Laughter: "Le Nain rouge"

> Si j'estois nain, j'aurais toute chose à souhait. . . .
> Puis qu'aujourd'huy les nains sont plus heureux que nous
> —Ronsard

THIS is a much darker variation on the theme of the outsider or freak. Its hero, who will end up as a sublime clown, is more sinister and much more ambivalent than Raphaël Bidoche, who in both his split guises is harmless. Lucien Gagneron is, until the climax, the archetypal malevolent dwarf.

In the present-day, well-meaning euphemism, this "alternatively-sized" man wears elevator shoes to increase his height from fifty to fifty-four inches. He is habitually angered by the mocking or pitying reactions of people of standard height. Such dwarfism, like sexism, racism, ageism, or any other form of human inhumanity, attempts to belittle the already small.[1] In mythology—though *Snow White* is the big exception—dwarfs, like gnomes, are generally regarded with fear as destructive creatures. Tom Thumb, le petit Poucet, is a rare instance of a kind miniature being. In society, midgets have for ages been exploited in sideshows and circuses. Tournier has admitted his debt to Selma Lagerlöf's *The Wonderful Adventures of Nils* (1906–7), where a boy is transmogrified into a dwarf by a blow from an offended gnome, and then benefits hugely from an enthralling tour of his native land on the back of a wild goose. "Le nanisme devient moyen d'évasion et instrument d'hyperconnaissance" (*VP*, p. 48). Of Günter Grass's *The Tin Drum* and its diminutive hero Oskar, Tournier states: "Le monde raconté par un nain—observé dans la *perspective de la grenouille,* selon une expression allemande consacrée [i.e., worm's-eye view]—c'est la voie ouverte à des aperçus bouleversants et dévastateurs" (*VV*, p. 336). In addition to such sources, the dwarf, as extended by Tournier, is also the inversion, the distorted mirror image, of the giant, the ogre. Lastly, Tournier's passion for children ensures that he treats those of similar height with aggressively protective affection.

Lucien's job prepares him for his later conquests. He brings an expertly sadistic talent to his work as a solicitor's clerk specializing in divorce cases. He is thus already exacting revenge for the lousy hand fate has dealt him. His current case concerns an ex-opera singer, Edith Watson, enriched by her first marriage to an American, and now in the process of divorcing her second husband Bob, a unisex giant, blond and gentle. It is significant that what Lucien most relishes in his hatchet job is the literary challenge of finding the most cutting words to describe the failed marriage, which are then fed into the couple's correspondence. As Tournier comments with pointed sarcasm, such poisonous letters enable partners to divorce "amicably" (*NR*, p. 104). Lucien excels himself, indeed goes over the top, in the letters he dictates to Bob, which include death threats. At this stage, then, Lucien exercises his destructive talents vicariously.

The discovery of the power of direct action over others starts when he visits the wife in her luxurious apartment. At first, she treats him like a nonentity, a fly. When, however, he goes to her lavish bathroom and sees his Lilliputian self multiplied in the profusion of mirrors, this narcissism cubed sets him off worshipping himself. Taking a shower he luxuriates in a kind of mini-orgy as the many jets spurt water at every portion of his anatomy. These ablutions are an erotic twist on the age-old idea of the purification rite. Lucien emerges a new person. For the first time in his life, he experiences his own flesh as a source of joy instead of disgust. He suddenly realizes he has untapped potentialities and, given his vengeful nature, he at once thinks in terms of dictatorial power. As in the commonplace view that small men—Hitler, Napoleon—lust to be tyrants, the worm turns. A further myth, that small men are incredibly sexy, ensures that Lucien is well-endowed. Indeed his sexual organs are described as hanging down to his knees, though of course his knees are nearer to his groin than in taller men. He has an ape-like appearance.

After the glorying, still mixed with some revulsion, in his own body comes the dressing up. Appropriately, Lucien selects a pur-

ple bathrobe, the imperial color. Thus decked, he is (oxymoronically) "un majestueux petit personnage" (p. 107). When he reappears before his client, he is not handsome, but disturbing, still comical but frightening. He is no longer a mere freak but "un monstre sacré" (ibid). It is Bob's robe he is wearing; he starts to supplant him. When Lucien and Edith come together in a sexual embrace, though virgin he performs superbly. He turns his handicap into an advantage once he assumes proudly his pygmy status and abandons his stacked heels. Like other Tournier figures, he makes a virtue (amoral) out of necessity. "Proscription vaut prescription."[2] Lucien is learning to have the courage of his convictions. Divorcing what sounds like an impotent or at least unsatisfying husband, Edith finds in her small lover extraordinary potency.[3] Thus begins a secret liaison between Edith and Lucien, who was already a double agent in his office. During their lovemaking, the former prima donna croons arias of sexual ecstasy, and mouths gleefully obscene words. She bends the term "ceinture de chasteté" to "ceinture de lubricité"; and to put this metaphor into practice, she carries Lucien strapped round her, like a young monkey (p. 108).

A sudden switch teams Bob and Edith up again. In accord with the legend of the fantastic strength packed into dwarfs, Lucien easily strangles his lover, with no premeditation. To cap the murder he possesses her dying body one last time; homicide and necrophilia conjoined. A sort of logic, of spontaneous destiny, has prevailed, which chimes with his deepest urges towards uncontested power. If he is some degree mad, and his ego system suggests he is, he retains crafty instincts of survival. He implicates Bob, recycling those useful letters and their death threats sent earlier, and forcing the innocent to go on the run.

Freedom from suspicion releases Lucien's mania. He begins to harbor monstrous dreams of genocide, imagining himself the commandant of a Nazi concentration camp for women, wielding the whip hand over huge flocks of naked, suffering, terrified females. He starts to hunger for public recognition of his exceptionality. Ordering a tight-fitting leotard which emphasises his biceps and genitals, he puts himself about, adopting the pose of a dangerous customer, rather like the *apaches* in fin-de-siècle Paris. (An old word for a dwarf was *dandiprat*). The normality of those he picks on in bars handicaps them, and, as Tournier relates else-

where, "la taille ramassée, les jambes courtes, les bras proportionellement longs, autant de facteurs qui, à défaut d'élégance, fournissent une assiette formidable dans le combat offensif et des atouts décisifs pour esquiver ou se dissimuler" (*VV*, p. 336). Lucien finds other bonuses: full-sized plates in restaurants give his meals ogrish dimensions. Men of normal height he terms *échassiers* (p. 113). In his eyes, they look like freaks on stilts and, expanding the chiasmus, he pictures their sex organs not as those of a gorilla like his, but marmoset-sized (*ouistitis*—the very word sounds disparaging).

As his notoriety spreads, he is approached by the Urbino circus manager. Though initially irked by what he takes as an insult, the job of a circus midget, Lucien suddenly thinks of the huge captive audience, and accepts. Traditionally, clowns stick at a problem, however ludicrous; they are physically pedantic, punctilious. Above all, and this is surely what appeals to Lucien, they enact what the spectators dare not do. Lucien makes the crowd laugh. Not the cruel laughter he has known most of his life, but the laughter of people enthralled. In line with the stereotype of womanly passivity, this is called "female laughter." He moves beyond this and like Robinson dreaming of transforming his body "en une main géante dont les cinq doigts seraient tête, bras et jambes" (*VLP*, p. 192), he devises a number where he dresses up as a giant hand on the end of a severed wrist. Tournier dwells on this uncanny, cavorting spectacle in *Le Vagabond immobile*:

> La rupture de la solidarité de la main et du corps. C'est l'image de la main coupée, vision d'horreur, et pire encore, la main coupée demeurée vivante, et qui court sur ses doigts. On a reconnu l'araignée dont la malédiction est d'être assimilée à une petite main sèche, amputée, mais douée d'une vélocité de cauchemar. (*VI*, p. 95)

Lucien's monstrous version cartwheels all over the arena. Yet even this does not satisfy him. He has made an object, a spectacle, only of himself. He needs a sidekick, so that he can make a spectacle of him, and in this way enshrine his own power.

Bob, conveniently, turns up. Tournier is never abashed about engineering coincidences. They form part of his special use of the word "logic." His heroes are more coherent than the norm; they assert themselves come hell or high water.[4] Lucien's megalomania logically needs a victim. Bob, who is born to victimhood, logically serves himself up to Lucien. The dwarf has the giant, desperate for a hiding place, in the palm of his hand. Tournier loves any turn-up for the book. To kick off, Lucien and Bob perform the most banally obvious act, David and Goliath, although Lucien mixes into the stockpot a comic extension in which he inflates Goliath into a blubbery mass which he prods all over the ring, and uses as a trampoline or punchball. The tiny adversary tames the colossus. A variant sees Lucien squatting on Bob's shoulders, as in the ancient topos of the dwarf astride the giant and seeing further than his mount. He drapes a long coat over Bob, converting this *échassier* into human stilts, while he himself lords it on high. This is power squared; his own strength plus borrowed support.

At school Tournier played the class clown, and at home listened avidly to Grock's records (*VP*, p. 38). Here he makes Lucien and Bob reenact the old circus opposition of the white-faced and the red-faced clowns, the posh and the boorish (already used in "Que ma joie demeure"). In a text on this tradition, Tournier argues that the white clowns resemble authors. They write their own material and so lay themselves more on the line than mere executants do. When, over the years, the white clown incorporated the red clown into his act, the coarse newcomer gradually stole the show from the would-be "aristocratic" white clown. Soon it was a moot point which was the stooge of which (see *VP*, pp. 33–36). Children especially love clowns because they mock authority, and children themselves adore face paint and pulling faces; they revel in knockabout farce.[5]

Just as in the circus tradition, the rough element has won out, so Lucien triumphs. He dolls up Bob in fancy clothes, and then torments and abuses him. The climax of this act is the grotesque mock wedding of the feminized Bob and the toadlike Lucien, who clings to the giant's body as earlier he had encircled Edith. A "natural" follow-up to this number is to possess Bob sexually. This pederastic phase comes next to last in the sequence, but is less important as a solution than as a revenge. There are very few happy couples in Tournier's work. Homosexuality is no more blissful an option than heterosexuality, though Tournier never castigates what is already socially disfavored. In addition, he has proposed that having several perversions makes them less dangerous as a whole than monomania. In all he writes, he works hard to persuade us that what many consider perversions are normal, harmless, or at least optional. This whole question is central also to "Le Fétichiste."

In his circus act with Bob, Lucien gives the imperial theme full rein, or reign. The red clown (l'Auguste) handily suggests Emperor Augustus. In fact, Augustus, like many monarchs up to the nineteenth century, kept a court dwarf, called Lucius. Augustus, however, is too respectable a role model for Lucien. He moves on to the infamous and eventually mad emperor Nero. Lucien Gagneron devises *le gag-Néron*, the Nero routine or visual gag. Bob plays Nero's suffering mother Agrippina, whom Nero murdered after committing incest with her. Lucien has selected an antihero.

"In traditional tales, dwarfs have no parents, nor do they marry or have children."[6] Lucien shocks Bob one night by exclaiming that his one disappointment is that together they can never beget a child. He decides to put on a special, free, children-only show, as juvenile laughter has always appeared to him the warmest and most innocent kind. As in "Que ma joie demeure," the show takes place on Christmas Eve. For once, the audience is the same height as himself. Cleverly, Tournier now leaves a gap in the narrative. The children-only show is their secret (young readers would love this touch). All we know is that Lucien wins an ovation, and afterwards the children carry him in triumph on their shoulders around the entire circus lot. When Bob bore Lucien, that was repressive power. When the children carry him, this is love, acceptance, shared joy. Tournier will not let go of *la phorie* which dominates *Le Roi des aulnes*. Lucien is of course still a dictator, but a benevolent despot now, indeed a comic dictator. Readers are requested to believe that, by some miracle of transfiguration, the monster Lucien has been saved, washed clean, just as at the start of his meteoric career he abluted himself ritually. He has regained, or achieved for the first time, innocence. Is this mere wishful thinking, a pious hope? The childlike side of Tournier means that he is more obsessed with innocence than with crime or sin. The circus owner values Lucien highly, and has found a slogan: "Lucius Gag-Néron, l'empereur des enfants!" Will Lucien rest content now; will he stop maltreating Bob? Can his crimes be so easily forgiven and forgotten, and the moral slate wiped clean? In terms of sexual preference, Lucien has shifted from virginity to heterosexuality, then pederasty, and finally to a special kind of paedophilia: a non-genital rejoicing in the contact with children. As Tournier says of paneroticism, playing on the sounds: "Toutes les voies et toutes les voix lui sont bonnes" (CS, p. 106).[7] Whether he creates dwarfs or ogres, Tournier gravitates to the monstrous, the whole hog. For him, purity is the real monstrosity: "Purification religieuse, épuration politique, sauvegarde de la pureté de la race" (RA, p. 125). Purists leech to stereotypes because they fear change or variety. Tournier exercises what Queneau called "the ducal privilege of neologising,"[8] whether it is actual coinages or refreshing the meaning of standard words. As well as *logique,* he relexicalizes *édification.* In Les Météores, Alexandre's hyperbolic dog Sam is cynically sodomizing a male dog already copulating with a bitch. This spectacle edifies Alexandre, "au double sens du mot, augmentant ma vertu, ma moralité, mais aussi ajoutant comme un étage au château de mes rêves par cet acte d'amour en seconde position" (M, p. 225). The second, amoral meaning obviously matters most to Tournier. Any lesson should be an extension, a new wing, rather than a reduction of possibilities via vetoes. Alexandre has the lordly grace to admit elsewhere that this view of the precious self as a permanent building site contains the danger of a Tower of Babel toppling over under its excess weight (M, p. 41).

Monsters are usually thought of as cautionary tales (*monere:* to warn), though Tournier favours the popular etymology (*monstrare:* to show). His dwarf finally makes a deliberate and enticing spectacle of himself instead of being, as at the outset, the passive recipient of other people's mockery. Whichever the derivation, monsters are over the top. They are either excessively pure, single-minded prodigies like Raphaël Bidoche, or excessively impure, mixed hybrids (e.g., opposite sexes blending as in androgynes). Like hybrids, monsters are generally sterile, as Lucien is with Bob. Does his fascination with monsters take Tournier himself over the top?

In *Le Vent Paraclet,* he describes his writing as a drawn out process of maturation, or in a more homely metaphor, a stewpot bubbling for ages while new ingredients are gradually added. Or again a house that he constructs painfully brick by brick around himself. At some point, this growing or cooking thing begins to escape his control. He then becomes its servant, or even its side-effect: the work leaves him standing, or for dead. What he detects in the whole process is a movement from quantity to quality, which he asserts can be observed in "Le Nain rouge" (*VP*, pp. 178–89). The spark that ignited this fable was his reading Sartre's *Les Mots* and the discussion there of small stature.[9] Sartre denies he is a dwarf. Tournier then began to speculate what the break-even point is between a dwarf and a small person. His own story, he claims, shows that a quantitative minus (a lack of inches) can lead to a qualitative plus (ibid., p. 180). Tournier has the grace to admit that his pleading is specious.[10] Is it indeed inevitable that quantity or size have anything to do with quality? Sexologists have tried to reassure numbers of anxious men on this score. Tournier acts forever the spin-doctor, and nowhere more than in his leitmotif of "l'inversion maligne-bénigne." This two-way shuttle engenders semiotic instability. "L'inversion maligne-bénigne, cette mystérieuse opération qui sans rien changer apparemment à la nature d'une chose, d'un être, d'un acte retourne sa *valeur*, met du plus où il y avait du moins, et du moins où il y avait du plus" (*VP*, p. 125). This assigning of new values, this rewriting of the actual, is the more existentialist aspect of Tournier's philosophy. He works back to front: "Pile est la vérité" (*VD*, n.p.). Behind all the inversions or changes of signs probably lurk the Christian ideas of reversibility of merits and compensation. Existentialist, crypto-Christian, but also ludic. When Abel Tiffauges finds out that a cherished body weighs incredibly light, he is converting gravity to levity (see *RA*, p. 133).[11] Tournier, in addition, inverts his own themes. After Abel, a microgenital giant, Lucien the well-hung dwarf.

Does Lucien get better the more strings he adds to his bow? Is not Tournier soft-pedalling on the ethical dimensions of his tale? If so, this is partly because he abominates orthodox moralizing, and partly because of his affinities with his hero. "J'obéis à une esthétique du merveilleux sordide."[12] As Tournier admits, with aplomb: "Après avoir fait le tour [du nain] objectivement et de l'extérieur, je me suis installé en son centre, décrivant dès lors le monde et les hommes à travers ses lunettes" (*VP*, p. 264). In general, Tournier impersonates his extremist figments so expertly that he runs the risk, gladly accepted, of being tarred with the same brush. Both Lucien and Tournier are artists. Each sets up his own system of order—and thus rivals God—his own patterns of cause-

and-effect. This imposition of order, however artificial (Lucien's universe is an elaborately *staged* one) brings fulfillment. The dwarf refuses his demeaned image; he makes something of himself; he takes pride in his size. This story is that of the artist as a dwarf, the dwarf as an artist. Notoriously unscrupulous, artists take their material where they find it, exploit everything and anyone. This may not be a pretty sight, but it does generate the amazing spectacle we call art.

9
Radio Daze and Imperishable Myth: "Tristan Vox"

> Radio is dreamlike, precognitive, primitive, ultimate. It has less to do with politics or society than with sex, nature, and religion ... A movie is just a picture, but people think radio is real.
> —G. Keillor

IN *Le Coq de bruyère,* the story "Tristan Vox" upturns the pattern of a more brutal partner, "Le Nain rouge." Its infelicitous hero comes to dread the power over thousands of others that comes his way. More usually captivated with signs and images than with sounds, Tournier has nevertheless on several occasions testified to his own state of thraldom when listening to broadcast voices. These both set the imagination flying and yet promote a strange sense of familiarity, what we could call the *déjà entendu.* From the active side of the microphone, Tournier recalls in well-rehearsed wonderment his broadcasting experience, where pathos and crypto-divinity rubbed shoulders:

> Mystère prodigieusement excitant, ... expérience capitale qui me faisait sentir la présence obscure mais vivante de cette hydre à un million de têtes, le "grand public." Expérience rendue plus bouleversante par le contact que j'eus un moment avec le courrier des auditeurs, cet énorme concert discordant, déchirant, grotesque, effrayant de voix de toutes provenances qui s'adressent à vous pour tout et pour rien, pour se plaindre en général de la maladie, du mari, ... de la malchance, ... de l'ennui, de la solitude, à vous ... qui peut tout, qui est ... Dieu. Oui, quiconque lit le courrier des auditeurs sonde toutes les plaies de ce monstre femelle et plaintif, la foule, et a une idée assez précise de ce que Dieu et ses saints entendent journellement dans les prières qui montent à eux. (*VP,* pp. 167–68)

"Tristan Vox" is a serio-comic tale of mass credulity. It displays an intense awareness of the awesome power of fabricated illusions, a power multiplied by the frantic acquiescence of the receivers.

For two reasons no doubt, Tournier accepts cheerfully from the outset the seeming risk of datedness involved in dwelling on the era of Radio Days (or Nights). Firstly, television is but a more recent variant on such illusionism; and radio, besides, still exerts a powerful appeal over large numbers of devotees. In his presentation of the days of radio monopoly, Tournier moots that abstracted voices encouraged in listeners unbridled flights of fancy. Listeners could make what they willed of those voices, or of the person projecting them. He draws an analogy with those religions where the voice of an invisible god is heard from on high. This will be the theme: the creation of a deity, the worshipping of a disembodied voice. In case such talk sounds far-fetched, we have only to recall the fully documented cultural phenomenon whereby a great many viewers or auditors convince themselves that imaginary characters in radio or television serials, soap operas, etc. are flesh-and-blood people, for whom wreaths are sent in when they are "killed off" by scriptwriters.

The pathetic protagonist of this tale is the eponymous Tristan Vox, a pseudonym suggesting blatantly both a melancholy delivery and the mythical hero of medieval literature. This voice has a dual effect on his mainly female audience: soothing/stimulating. The voice of the ideal lover perhaps: faithful and reliable, but exciting. It sounds as if it bears some secret sorrow or wound. It has a catch in it, "une fêlure, une cassure" (*TV*, p. 126). At this stage, then, the hero has a crack in his voice. Later he will watch a crevasse gape open in his very personality and being.

The anonymity, the facelessness, of radio enables this voice to be all things to all women. And yet the image that collects around it betrays an amazing consensus. It is as if thousands were dreaming the same dream. The mass media can still exploit the hardy vestiges of the courtly love tradition (*amor de lonh*, quite literally): "Tristan Vox, superbe assemblage de roman courtois et de modernisme vulgaire" (p. 129). That collective image is of a mature, sad-looking man with romantically long chestnut hair. It bears little relation to the actual owner of the voice, Félix Robinet. Félix (misnamed the fortunate one) contrasts with Tristan, and *robinet* is the most common of household objects. Félix is nearly sixty, bald, short and potbellied. His voice is the by-product of recurrent laryngitis and a wobbly double chin. After an earlier life as a comic thespian touring the provinces, he has settled into a comfortable life on the radio and his cozy bourgeois home.

His first job had been that of the Speaking Clock on the telephone, but his distinctive voice immediately captured the public interest. What or who lay hidden behind it? The pseudo-mystery was of course stoked up by the tabloid press, obsessed by the overlap between media personalities and private lives. By nature mistrustful of change, lacking in ambition and rather pessimistic in outlook, Félix is initially very dubious when his employer tells him his voice is worth a fortune. He endorses the plan, however, which is to keep his private life secret, and to let his broadcast self work its wonders. It is, Félix reflects, a funny old fate. On stage in the past, his voice had moved nobody. He accepts, then, trying to imagine that no real harm will ensue. The omniscient teller here anticipates the latter part of the story, justifiably, for it is the story of a destiny; a process, once set in motion, will prove unstoppable. The imaginary will not be kept at a safe distance, but will gradually vampirize reality, and indeed replace it. Myth will become Félix's daily bread.

It is like a fairy tale, but of the kind where things go awry, e.g., "The Sorcerer's Apprentice," where the tyro cannot control the magic powers that he unleashes. Félix does not in fact have to slave in order to weave his magic: it just happens. What does he talk about in his solo chat shows? This and that. In fact, he talks about things he has no experience or possession of: gardens, pets. As such, he emulates those authors who write of imagined events rather than from firsthand experience. If this is lying, then actors (which Félix was) are also liars: they embody nonexistent characters. The difference between Tristan Vox and a stage actor is that Tristan claims, implicitly, in his broadcasts that he is who he sounds like; he makes himself up as he goes along, instead of interpreting a script devised by someone else. Obviously, all these are potentially dangerous games, as any swivelling between reality and illusion can become. Tristan does not as yet realize that he is playing with dynamite.

Even his secretary, the "scrawny, horse-faced" Mlle. Flavie (p. 131), finds it hard to disentangle Félix Robinet from Tristan Vox. It is always a great relief for Félix to escape from the studio late at night and hurry home for a late meal with his wife Amélie, a superb cook; there he feels safe. His wife, née Lamiche, embodies like a loaf of bread warmth, nourishment, security. The would-be earth-bound Tristan, well stoked by his wife's peasant Auvergnat cuisine, fears, unlike many another Tournier protagonist, being immaterialized. The first set of fan letters he receives are gastronomical in flavor, and disclose intimate knowledge of his origins and his domestic life. They are signed Yseut. Tristan wonders whether the microphone he speaks into transmutes his voice by some diabolic means. It is, after all, shaped like a serpent's head. His studio strikes him as a tomb from which, as in several mythologies including the Christian, a new creature arises in a process of death and rebirth. (The same pattern occurs in another story of perverse initiation, in Le Coq de bruyère, "Les Suaires de Véronique.") Tristan's broadcasts are a bridge between two insular solitudes, his own and that of his vast unseen audience—a situation akin to that of the writer Tournier, addressing unknown readers from his study.

The letters from Yseut grow more and more erotic, obscene even, and come accompanied by explicit drawings. The approach is thus two-pronged: after *l'estomac, le bas-ventre*. Then fate introduces a new twist, a more excruciating turn of the screw. In the equivalent of *Radio Times*, an editor mistakenly prints Tristan Vox's name under the photo of a tennis star, Frédéric Durâteau.[1] A face now exists to go with the legendary name. Félix's "Tristan Vox" has been usurped by a rival, however unintentionally. Félix, the genuine fake, working under a pseudonym, begins to feel like a real impostor; and the mind starts to boggle. Durâteau complains that his life is being wrecked and that it is somehow Félix's fault. The reader may well feel at this point that poor Félix is the only remotely sane person in a gallery of fruit cases. We might also wonder whether ordinariness is meant to appear as just a variant form of monstrosity. Being the odd man out, even if you are approximately in the right, puts you out on a limb, beyond the pale.

Events accelerate and escalate. Mlle. Flavie jumps or falls out of a third-floor window, and lies in intensive care. When Félix rushes to visit her, she murmurs through her grotesque bandages that she has a confession to make. She is Yseut. Or rather that she took over from the original Yseut (as Durâteau supplanted Félix). She had wanted desperately to see the legendary Tristan come real. All around Félix, people are recycling the Tristram and Isolde myth. In "Tristan Vox," fate dominates individuals and their relationship with others; they have small say in their own destinies. On display is not conjugal fidelity, of slender interest to Tournier, but faithfulness to a fateful, pre-scripted passion, updated.

On his return home, Amélie confesses to Félix that she is Yseut. Hearing her husband's voice over the radio waves had created a being different from the man she lived with. She had written letters in the guise of Yseut in order to win back the man whose life was being stolen from him and her by all his unseen admirers. The only solution he can imagine is to cut off the supply of the narcotic, "fermer le robinet," as he says in a wry pun on his own name. He requests leave; his wife and he go back to their roots in central France. Amélie, however, has lost all interest in cooking, that is, in Félix as a bodily person. One night he catches her listening with a friend to the radio: Tristan Vox, now impersonated totally by Frédéric Durâteau. The story breaks off when Félix spots the name Tristan Vox on an envelope about to be posted, on the sly, by Amélie. She has not been cured of her delusion. For his part, will Félix himself ever escape from his phantom? The Tristan myth, in Tournier's view, is one of stasis and therefore of repetition (*VV*, p. 37).

This story shares with "Le Coq de bruyère" the theme of aging sexuality—Mlle. Flavie, Amélie, and the hordes of largely female listeners. Félix's audience has in effect derealized him.[2] What state he ends up in is left to our putative compassion to imagine. He has suffered an existential split between his voice and the whole rest of his self. In addition, an interloping double, Durâteau, has taken over Félix's persona. Tournier's exploitation of the ancient Doppelgänger topos is largely joco-serious in its modernization of an old myth. As Ruthven says of such myth-conversion: "Operating within a network of shared allusions among educated readers, you can by-pass the explicit in order to explore the tacit and ironic."[3]

In answer to a question as to whether he is possessed by myths, Tournier punned in agreement, "si cela peut aussi vouloir dire bouffé aux mites." He went on to say that writing drains the author, renders him threadbare.[4] The creative hack becomes hackneyed. This process is reflected in the dematerialization of Félix. Many have always suspected that a goodly number of myths originate in some form of wordplay. At different times Tournier writes identically of myths and humor that each is "un rappel au désordre" (see *VP,* pp. 191ff, and *VV,* p. 35). Since, for Tournier, myths need to be periodically reinvented or invested with new meaning, twisting them for reuse is as central to creativity as is punning. Like fables, symbols or puns, myths are always **tantamount,** suggestive (Tournier would say "apéritif") rather than definitive. In his view, myths provide an already constituted meaning, or set of variant meanings—*le donné*—which latercomers can make something of by hijacking, adapting, inverting, etc. (*le construit*).[5]

Tournier is taken with both kinds of rustling, the plagiaristic and the auditory, as in "ce bruissement mythologique, ce bain d'images dans lequel vivent [les contemporains de l'artiste]" (*VP,* p. 192).

All in all, for Tournier myth is ambivalent (or multivalent):

> La notion même de mythe est frappée d'équivoque: un mythe, c'est à la fois une belle et profonde histoire incarnant l'une des aventures essentielles de l'homme, et un misérable mensonge débité par un débile mental, un "mythomane" justement. (*VV,* p. 14)

The "débile mental" in "Tristan Vox" is no doubt the national audience creating its pathetic falsehoods about Félix Robinet. And yet, from another angle, and like "Les Suaires de Véronique," this story could be read as women's revenge match.

> Les femmes d'aujourd'hui se révoltent assez contre l'image de la femme-objet, répandue par nos mass media, précieuse, passive, déshabillée, maquillée, photographiée, vendue en effigie ou en chair et en os. Le mythe de Tristan fait de l'homme un objet aussi, sans cesse ballotté, endommagé et raccommodé par des mains de femme. (*VV,* p. 30)

Tournier's gesture towards asserting women's rights here secretes some traditional male stereotypes of women; and his sympathies clearly go to the endangered cynosure.

Just as Véronique in "Les Suaires de Véronique" could stand for any manipulatrix, so Félix is an (unwilling) dictator of the airwaves, swaying masses.[6] This story is also a typically ambivalent attack on modern commercial media, for their ability to concoct a synthetic product (the ersatz, Durâteau, serves just as well as the "original," Félix), and to wash their hands of any disastrous consequences. The new order created by art, even low-grade art like radio chat shows, cannot always be kept under control. Unlike Lucien Gagneron in "Le Nain rouge," the artist here is at the mercy of his audience. Unlike Raphaël Bidoche in "Que ma joie demeure," he experiences the wrong kind of acclaim. Like Tupik, on the other hand, Félix suffers a mutilation; he is cut down to his voice alone. Tournier has often claimed, with variable plausibility, that at some point his books escape his grasp. Like Tristan Vox, Tournier must sometimes feel that his real self has become a public cliché, a corny figment in the collective semiconscious of his public.

Tournier's "Gothic" version of author-reader relationships shuttles confusingly between images of books as vampires feeding off the lifeblood of readers, but also sucking the writer himself dry. More phallocentrically, books are cocks mounting a production line of hens: us readers.[7] By one of those changearounds of signs that so fascinate Tournier, the reader (seen also at times as a vampire) can become a mere sucker, or dupe. "Tristan Vox" houses not only the polymorphous eroticism that surfaces continuously in Tournier's fiction, but also the dependence, the aggression, the scorn and the need that variously constitute his attitude to his readership.

10
Photographic Fetishism: "Les Suaires de Véronique"

Though "Tristan Vox" centers on a radio performer, it implicitly suggests also photography, as it is concerned with images; the late-night studio resembles a darkroom where Tristan's imposed image is developed. The imaginary distorts the real. These themes are given astounding extensions in "Les Suaires de Véronique." *Le Roi des aulnes,* and other texts, had already stressed the sadism inherent in photography. In *Le Roi des aulnes,* the predatory Abel Tiffauges obsessively shoots the "perfect" wound on the knee of a young skater, to the extent of cuffing the lad to force him upright for the pose. Unlike Véronique, however, Tiffauges is capable also of gentleness, for he later carries the boy to medical attention.[1] Tournier often refers to photography as rape.[2] Indeed, people in many cultures evade being photographed, for fear that their self may be stolen. "Les Suaires de Véronique" relates the protracted violation, body and soul, of a man by a woman.

It has a real-life setting, the annual international jamboree for photographers in Arles. Just like Tournier, however, who is anything but an orthodox realist in his fictions, Véronique seeks to go one, or several, better than reality, to attain ultrarealism in her photographs. She wants nothing less than to abolish the frontiers between the subject of a photo and the recorded image itself: to fuse the two into one.

The narrator, who has a louche part to play in the story, first sees Véronique and her guinea-pig-to-be, Hector, in a particularly legendary stretch of Provence, the Camargue—swamps and lagoons, herds of wild bulls and mustangs. It is nowadays a mixture of nature reserve, tourist trap, bullfighting Spain, and the Wild West of the U.S. (there are dude ranches). It is also a land of local

10: PHOTOGRAPHIC FETISHISM: "LES SUAIRES DE VÉRONIQUE"

myths about fabulous creatures or monsters, and of Greco-Roman traditions. Sea, soil, sand, saltwater expanses, burned in summer by a relentless sun.

The narrator's first view of Hector is of a superb, naked body, wading through the waters, or stretched out on the sand, or curled up in a fetal position, while a group of photographers machine gun him with their cameras. Hector seems a sun-and-water god, powerful-looking though with a childish air; a magnificent hunk, apparently mindless. His only apparel is a large tiger's tooth, a seemingly virile emblem, on a leather lace around his neck. (He later explains that this is an Indian lucky charm to protect the wearer against being eaten by tigers. It will play a dramatic role in the story.) He welcomes the attention of the photographers with a kind of self-adoration. He is blatantly another of Tournier's narcissists.

The photographer Véronique, on the other hand, is not pretty, but is full of feverish energy and quick-tempered. She dismisses derisively the banal shots taken of Hector by the others: *clichés*, in both French senses. Prophetically, she declares: "Ce petit Hector, on aimerait en faire quelque chose" (*SV*, p. 155). She adds that that would entail a great deal of work and sacrifice. *Travail* also means ordeal, and in fact comes from the Latin *tripalium*, an instrument of torture. ("Si profonde est parfois la sagesse que recouvre une parenté verbale" (*VLP*, p. 65).[3] Véronique will work over, torture Hector so as to engender a new creature. Dissatisfied with the given man, she wants to reshape, indeed recreate him. There have been many myths of men wishing to remodel women to fit their own plan for them. This story is a revenge match (cf. "Tristan Vox"), which resituates Véronique in another ancient tradition: woman as witch. The stereotyped sex roles are reversed. Véronique is dominant, Hector largely docile. When the narrator returns for the next annual gathering, he finds Véronique unchanged but Hector barely recognizable, grown alarmingly thin. Ever ready to gloss her doings, Véronique agrees that, when she found him, Hector was beautiful but not, in her special use of the term, "photogenic" (p. 156). By this she means photos which go further than the mere real-life model. Her kind of photos seek to create a new beauty and are, indeed, she boasts, more beautiful than the person posing for them. Art takes over from life and operates separately, and better.

She has in effect sequestered Hector in a small country house. This is the setting for her experiment in a variant form of vivisection, an operation on the living flesh. The whole space of the house is devoted either to photography or to exercise equipment, in order to make and keep Hector's body as athletically perfect as possible. Without evincing much disapproval, the narrator finds the house a mixture of operating theater and torture chamber. Véronique has got rid of all flab, has reduced Hector to what she believes to be his essence. It is ambiguous whether he is now a living skeleton or a sculptural marvel. The year before he had appeared a child of nature. Now he is an antinatural production. As he lies asleep in his egg-shaped shell of a room, he is being prepared for an artificial rebirth (*renaissance*). We will see later how obsessed Véronique is with certain anatomical practices of the Renaissance. Many religions demand from their acolytes a rite of entry, a dying to the past and a rebirth.

"Par la tête, le corps est spiritualisé, désincarné, éludé" (*RA*, p. 539). Véronique delivers a harangue, a sermon on the montage. She stresses the primary importance of the face, and mentions how many nude photographs have been spoilt by inappropriate faces. Lucien Clergue resolved this dilemma, she explains, in a radical way by omitting the heads of his models: decapitated nudes. In her view, this amputation forces greater intensity on to the trunk and limbs, as there is no distraction. While she believes this to be great art, she thinks it works only for female nudes. A headless and therefore faceless male nude is ruined. The narrator makes only bland objections to her views, which habitually ride roughshod. Véronique adds that she is not talking about the need for an intelligent-looking face on top of a male body (and Hector hardly shines in this area). That too would distract, like a lighthouse lantern, as she puts it (p. 159). She wants, in effect, a mindless male face. She shows the narrator a photo of Hector, which calls to his mind insects pinned to a case by a collector. By very severe lighting and by isolating Hector against a totally black background, she has, it appears, stripped him to the bone, dissected him as in an autopsy. By now more ill at ease, the narrator comments that this photo does not look like a life study, *du pris sur le vif*. Véronique readily admits that mere exact photographic reproduction of appearances does not interest her. She quotes the

10: PHOTOGRAPHIC FETISHISM: "LES SUAIRES DE VÉRONIQUE"

words of Paul Valéry: "'La vérité est nue, mais sous le nu, il y a l'écorché'" (p. 160): flayed flesh.

Véronique distinguishes two main types of photography: one memorably captures fleeting moments that speak of the universal human condition which, she adds lugubriously, comes out of nothing and finally returns there. The other sets up, in a calculated and artificial fashion, something far more static and eternal. Preferring the stationary to the mobile, Véronique opts against ordinary living. The narrator's gloss is: on the one side "life study" (*pris sur le vif*) and on the other "still life" (*nature morte*). Or, he goes on, ludically crisscrossing: *la nature vive* (the world as it is, in flux), and on the other *le pris-sur-le-mort* (p. 161). Not life-studies, but death-studies. Véronique admits the fascination of death, and says she will probably end up taking pictures in a morgue. She is especially taken with what she terms the "weight" of death. A corpse, for her, is like a marble slab; she compares it with a child who resists being picked up and who becomes a "dead weight" (ibid.).

She links her fixation on death with the art of the Renaissance which, in her view, truly discovered the beauty of cadavers, of still, dead flesh. Classical Greek art had been based on exact observation of living bodies, especially athletes. Véronique's culture-hero is Andreas Vesalius, a sixteenth-century researcher from Flanders, who dared to dissect corpses, an act vetoed by law and by religion. Among the artists of the period, Leonardo da Vinci and Benvenuto Cellini produced anatomical plates, and others were fascinated by skinned bodies.

Such obsessions in Véronique seem morbid, and she eagerly accepts the charge. When, recalling the Spanish Inquisition, the narrator asks her whether she might not have died at the stake if she had lived in that age, she replies that the really canny witches of that time made sure they were members of the Inquisition. Clearly, while she is prepared to immolate Hector, she has no urge to martyrize herself. Indeed, her posture is forever on the sidelines, out of reach and, in the end, literally getting away with murder.

Hector has been speechless (*infant*) so far. He sleeps while they talk. Véronique's regime for him is: little food and lots of sleep. She quotes the old proverb: "Qui dort dîne."[5] She wants him to feed off the same imaginary fare as herself, and so keeps him just this side of starvation. Tournier frequently stresses her possessive gaze. Hector is her creature: she is rivalling God. Indeed, the model does most of the work, while the artist stands aloof, like a certain God, paring her fingernails.

Yet a few days later, the narrator finds Véronique in a sleazy bar, much the worse for drink. Hector has fled, and she shows the farewell letter. Hector has kept a count. She has taken ("arraché," he says) 22,239 photos of him over the past thirteen months. A rape and a robbery; he has been "plucked like a chicken."[6] None of this would have happened, he accuses her, if she had not stolen his magic talisman, the tiger's tooth. Though he is now just skin and bone, "Vous n'aurez pas ma peau" (p. 166). The letter is mindlessly optimistic. Hector should have known Véronique better than this. As he has repossessed his lucky charm, he feels, stupidly, safe.

For the first time, the narrator seems to veer towards Hector's side, when he lets slip that he thinks of Véronique as a tigress ready to devour her prey. He has (it is his turn to give a minilecture) done some boning-up on Vesalius in the local library. That Renaissance man haunted cemeteries, scaffolds, hospitals, torture chambers, in order to observe death in all its manifestations. Still very blandly, the narrator adds that such activities would have been horrifying, if they had not been "purified by the light of Vesalius' intellect" (p. 167). Vesalius progressed from cutting up corpses to vivisection of the bodies of drugged prisoners. The narrator's litotic comment? "C'est un peu rude" (p. 168). Vesalius was condemned to death for his illegal experiments, but got off and died in exile. There is something ethically fishy about the narrator's backing up of Véronique via this spot of research. She is impressed by this edifying potted biography.[7] Domineering discourse suits her to a T.

The narrator next hears of her back in Paris from a gossip, Chériau. Véronique has recaptured her quarry, and started experiments in what she calls "direct photography," i.e., without a camera, film or use of enlarger. Just as she offloaded her pile of cameras on the narrator at their first meeting, all her efforts involve moving beyond material reality which she finds an encumbrance. She is pursuing some kind of pure, disembodied essence—an idea, really, of the perfect image. In her own way, she practices a form of sublimation or abstraction. In her new mode, she takes photographic paper and exposes it to daylight, which turns it slightly yellow. She then plunges Hector in a bath of developing fluid. She lays him, dripping, on to the treated paper in the posture she has selected. Finally, she fixes the image he has imparted directly on to the paper, and sends Hector off to shower.[8] Reporting Véronique's own boastful words, Chériau says that the resulting two-dimensional projection of Hector's body resembles the images, blasted into the walls of Hiroshima, of Japanese bodies subjected to extreme doses of radiation. A "direct photograph," a transfer of flesh to paper.

Tournier has written on the artist Yves Klein, whose "Anthropométries" involved the daubing of models in blue paint who then imprinted themselves directly on to sheets of paper. A variant series was executed on cloth and called "Suaires." Tournier has denied any influence, yet writes of Klein's body art: "Il n'hésite pas à [le] rapprocher du voile de Véronique et aussi des silhouettes humaines imprimées dans la pierre des rues et des murs d'Hiroshima par la bombe atomique."[9] Was Tournier lying in his teeth, to no very useful end? Or is this a further example of would-be lordly unconcern, blithe piracy? If he suffers from what Harold Bloom calls "anxiety of influence," he hides it very well. Indeed, he can sound like a Pataphysician claiming "anticipatory plagiarism" on the part of the victim of larceny. In *Les Météores*, Alexandre recounts the theory of the recycler Briffaut:

> Le père Briffaut m'a exposé un jour sa théorie de l'objet perdu, de la chose sans maître qu'il considère comme sa propriété personnelle—de plein droit, par privilège professionnel—avant même de l'avoir trouvée ... quiconque la trouve avant lui est coupable de vol. (*M*, pp. 211–12).

Rosello states:

> On retrouve ce besoin, constant dans l'oeuvre de Tournier, du second degré, de la copie, de la copie de la copie, de l'acte de réécriture et de relecture, activités qui permettent la création à partir du déjà créé et court-circuitent ainsi la nécessité de la procréation.[10]

Tournier does not talk, like many another writer of either gender, of his books as his children, but as his excrement. Scatology excites him erotically and aesthetically, as when he has Tiffauges exclaim: "Je regarde attendri ce beau poupon dodu de limon vivant que je viens d'enfanter"(*RA,* p. 144). Procreation displaced to defecation.

Of course, Hector does not escape Véronique's treatment, her reconversion of him, unscathed. He has been hospitalized with a skin disease over his entire epidermis. Stigmata are an ambidextrous concept over historical time: holy marks, or the identifying brand of slaves and criminals in ancient Greece or Rome. Chériau concludes his account by predicting that, if Hector does not get away from this witch soon, she will finally "avoir sa peau." That idiom is getting ever closer to coming literally true. As in "Le Coq de bruyère," we see here the mythopoeic power of a pun, whereby it generates or controls a whole text. The word or phrase comes first. The justification or extension follows suit.[11]

Later, and "rituellement," the narrator returns to Arles, where Véronique has an exhibition. In the program, she explains that she has moved on again, from paper to cloth, to shrouds in fact. As before steeped in developing fluid, the model is laid on photosensitive cloth, and the image is fixed. This operation produces intriguing effects, especially if the model is first painted with other chemicals. The result is unusual shades of blue and gold. In Véronique's view, the term "photography" should be supplanted by "dermography" (p. 171). She in fact *lifts* Hector, in three senses: she purloins him; she transfers his image; but she believes she is elevating him, or more importantly herself, on to a higher plane of achievement.[12] Tournier who, when he returned from study in Germany in 1950, felt "vraiment irrésistible, le Popeye de la philosophie,"[13] believed then (and possibly believes now) that: "il dépend de notre seule force cérébrale de concevoir des ensembles d'un degré de cohérence supérieur au 'réel' et donc d'un degré de réalité plus élevé"(*VP,* p. 157).

The narrator visits the exhibition in the nave of a disused chapel. Véronique is indeed inaugurating a substitute religion of photographic art. Her "shrouds" are draped all round the walls. Each plays variations on body postures: flattened, magnified, curled up (as in Hector's fetal position at the outset or when asleep), unrolled. Without naming Nazi extermination camps, the narrator is reminded of sets of human skins torn off and displayed as trophies. The atmosphere is stiflingly oppressive; he feels as if he were in a morgue. *Morgue* is a handy double meaning, a black

10: PHOTOGRAPHIC FETISHISM: "LES SUAIRES DE VÉRONIQUE" 69

pun: mortuary, and insane pride. Though rather sickened, the narrator is not fully disgusted, because he is a kissing cousin to Véronique, and because he recalls schoolboys' cruel games of squashing flies with the fist between two sheets of paper in order to get an imprint of the body. Véronique's obsession, in all its inhuman, gory glory, is on public show: Hector is plastered all over the walls. The narrator has time only to ask Véronique before she leaves what she has done with Hector. Her enigmatic reply is to gesticulate towards all the imprinted shrouds. "Hector. Mais il est ... J'en ai fait ... ça. Que voulez-vous de plus?" (p. 172). Before he can ask more, he spots the tiger's tooth on its lace around her neck. There is now only silence. We must conclude that she has definitively devoured her prey, and had Hector's skin. It has been a very unequal contest.

The mention of shrouds calls to mind the Shroud of Turin, a relic believed by some to be the linen cloth used to wrap Christ's body for burial. It bears impressions of a human body marked with wounds consonant with those sustained by Christ at the Crucifixion. Some scientists maintain it is a medieval fake. A related matter is the significance of the name Véronique. Tournier comments in these terms on Veronica's meeting with Jesus on his way to Calvary:

> Le nom de cette femme pieuse de Jérusalem veut dire; image vraie [*vera* + *icon*]. Véronique a essuyé avec son voile le visage ruisselant de sang, de larmes et de sueur du Sauveur. Et le miracle s'est produit: le visage de Jésus imprima son image sur le voile de Véronique. C'est elle, une femme, et nul autre—ni Nièpce, ni Daguerre—qui a inventé l'image vraie, l'image photographique. (*CM*, p. 172)[15]

Quoting "Love thy neighbour as thyself," Tournier wonders in another text on photography: "Y aurait-il une affinité secrète entre le miroir d'eau de Narcisse et le voile de Véronique?"[16] If so, it is a one-way mirror, for Tournier's Véronique is a narcissist, light years from the female good Samaritan. She is in fact unsaintly, misnamed, as is the unheroic Hector. For Roberts, she is "une inversion maligne" of her legendary forerunner.[17] A further area of reference is to the bullfight. The Camargue near Arles is the home of wild bulls, and Arles stages corridas in its Roman arena. Hector is described as built like a bullock. Véronique plays this inexperienced creature for a long time, torments him, weakens him, dominates him, and finishes him off. The classic bullfighter's pass with the large cape is *la verónica*. The whole corrida is a ritual display and execution.

Both feminists and male chauvinists could find ammunition for their causes in this story. As in "Tristan Vox," a man is imprisoned by domineering female attention. In "Le Nain rouge," the woman carries the prodigiously equipped dwarf on her hip, like a baby; he may give her pleasure, but she annexes it and him. In "Le Coq de bruyère," the wife outlives the husband in wholeness and vigor. Véronique "a la peau d'Hector." "Les Suaires de Véronique" is an unedifying parable about all manipulators and dictators. It is about fanaticism, taking desires to absurd, lethal ends. A branch of fanaticism is fetishism. Véronique pursues an erotics of seeing: the eye possesses what other parts cannot or do not want to reach; she whores after strange gods. She inverts the stereotype of fashion photography:

> Dialogue muet de la femme, coléoptère exhibé à la pointe d'une épingle,—c'est bien cela que veut dire *pin-up girl*,—et du fétichiste invisible, inventif, impérieux, souvent homosexuel, fermement décidé à mortifier cette chair autant que l'exigera son âpre passion. (CS, p. 82)

He quotes as an example:

> les photos de Sieff,—qui sont comme l'éclatement de l'image de mode,—nous suggèrent de donner au mot *chic* une ampleur nouvelle. Le *chic* devrait devenir le principe d'une morale, d'une érotique, d'une religion, d'une métaphysique. Principe où il y aurait du contournement et de la torture, car on n'oublie pas que *chic* vient étymologiquement de *chicane*. (CS, P. 84)[18]

There are many fearful male myths about voracious women, likened to the praying mantis which consumes its mate; the *vagina dentata* hardly bears thinking about.

Tournier found the television film based on his story not hot or fleshly enough. The reason, he felt, was the self-censoring that producers practice in order to get their works on the small screen and, beyond that, the contemporary morality which endorses violence but jibs at "l'amour réel, profond."[19] Love seems hardly the word for the relationship between Hector and Véronique who, incidentally, were played as Jewish and German characters respectively.

Véronique is a totally unscrupulous artist who inscribes her own vision on the skin, the blank page, of Hector. Apart from solidarity with a fellow artist, the narrator, while querying and ribbing Véronique at times, has another reason for not outrightly condemning her. Tournier has proudly confessed that he too has an obsession with opened-up flesh, wounds, scarred tissue, etc. "L'arrachement d'un pansement qui découvre la gueule rose et goinfrée d'une cicatrice toute fraîche, cela va tout de même plus loin qu'un banal strip-tease." Forgetting his own traumatic tonsillectomy, he wonders why we do not exploit "les ressources érotiques de la chirurgie? . . . La troublante beauté des blessures et le fantasque cérémonial d'une salle d'opération."[20]

> Le corps humain, blessé, saigné, tué et mis en linceul, grand thème qui remue en chacun de nous des vertiges métaphysiques et des ivresses sado-masochistes . . . Le pansement prend la relève du drapé classique, plus intime, plus équivoque, puisqu'il habille non la nudité, mais la plaie. (CS, p. 79)

Such passages reveal Tournier testing himself, and even more his readers, as to how much horror, how many twists, can be stomached. His imaginative sympathies lie with those who go over the top, "qui forcent la dose." Because of her monolithic nature, devoid of inner splits, Véronique is the one true monster, in any sense, in Tournier's work. One reason why Alexandre in *Les Météores* is so winning, or at least engaging, is that he is self-undermined. We readers prefer broken-backed to ramrod creatures. Véronique plays God in his stiffest avatar. Yet, Tournier realistically recognizes the dangers of obsession with images, whether acoustic as in "Tristan Vox" or pictorial as here in "Les Suaires de Véronique." The danger in the long run is, most profoundly, that it is that long run up to the disastrous end that most intrigues him.

For one critic, Weightman, this story could be an updating, a "creative parody," of Poe's story "The Oval Portrait," "in which a painter drains off all life from a young girl as his depiction of her becomes more vital."[21] As in Flaubert's "Hérodias," (much beloved of Tournier) something has to be sacrificed before something greater can be created. Aristotle's version, used as epigraph to Queneau's *Zazie dans le Métro,* is "Ho plasas ephanisen": the artist fabricated and abolished.[22] Hector has been Véronique's raw material. He starts off naked, and he ends up skinned alive. It is hard to imagine Véronique resting on her laurels. Where can she possibly go next? There is, of course, an unrealized and ironic aftermath: Hector will last longer, at least in his imaged form, than the end-stopped Véronique. True images, however callously obtained, outlive Veronicas.

11

Something about Nothing: "La Jeune Fille et la mort"

> I sometimes feel that I have nothing to say and I want to communicate this.
> —Damien Hirst, sculptor

LICHTENBERG sported ponderously with nothing: "A leg of mutton is better than nothing, nothing is better than Heaven, therefore a leg of mutton is better than Heaven."[1] More to my present point, Swift: "I am trying an Experiment very frequent among Modern Authors; which is, to write upon Nothing."[2] This could be a prescient comment on the possibly postmodernist games of Michel Tournier. In what he called his after-sales manual, *Le Vent Paraclet,* during a disquisition on "cosmic laughter," Tournier states: "Lorsque les lattes disjointes de la passerelle où chemine l'humanité s'entrouvrent sur le vide sans fond, la plupart des hommes ne voient rien, mais certains autres voient le rien." (*VP,* p. 199)

The name of the young protagonist of "La Jeune Fille et la mort," Mélanie Blanchard, is, as so often in Tournier's work, loaded. *Melas* in Greek means black (as in melancholia); and Blanchard is self-explanatory. Her name, like that of Raphaël Bidoche in "Que ma joie demeure," is an oxymoron, a yoking of opposites. Tournier's favorite form of photography is black-and-white, which he claims is capable of subtler effects than color photography. Initially virgin, Mélanie will be ultimately and with a smile on her face raped by death.

The tale begins at school, a mainly unhappy series of places in Tournier's autobiographical account, offset only by his willful playing of the class clown. Mélanie too is something of a sore thumb, an odd girl out, though not in any provocative way. Tournier, in fact, can define her only negatively: "ni difficile, ni secrète, ni mélancolique" (*JFM*, p. 181). Obviously bright, she has strange habits such as sucking lemons during lessons. She has macabre interests. In history, she is drawn to famous people who were tortured and executed: Joan of Arc, Gilles de Rais, Mary Stuart, Charles I, Damiens.

The set topic of her latest essay is the stock "What I did in my holidays." She chooses a family picnic, which had to be cancelled owing to the sudden death of the grandmother. From this (fictional) opening onwards, the whole exercise is ruled by negation: the non-audition of birdsong, the non-return under a storm, the non-drying of clothes. A non-event, an exercise in imagination, which indeed often negates and offers an alternative version of reality, as Philip Larkin illustrates:

> And here we have that splendid family
> I never ran to when I got depressed,
> The boys all biceps and the girls all chest...
> The bracken where I never trembling sat,
> Determined to go through with it; where she
> Lay back, and "all became a burning mist"...
>
> "Nothing, like something, happens anywhere."[3]

As Auden noted, "Poetry makes nothing happen."[4] Like Larkin, Mélanie is saying: "No, nothing happened." Like him, she is writing against cliché—though her essay begins "assez banalement" (p. 176)—against the same old story. Her negative invention is comic; death is from the outset wedded to laughter. Gravely, and all the more funnily for that, Mélanie joshes the whole ritual of school essays, family outings and grandmas turning their toes up. In the remainder of the story, her obsession with death will be rarely gloomy, most often excited and jubilant. In cancelling itself out, her essay asserts itself. Mélanie has quite literally, like the archetypal great artist, made something out of nothing, by an act of bravura against imposition.

The teacher is perplexed by this performance, as by the lemons. What do the disparate clues add up to? The answer, unavailable to the teacher but to which the reader is privy, is that Mélanie is bored. Not just run-of-the-mill boredom, but an essentially philosophical acedia. A kind of nausea, a sickening gray tide, covers everything, threatening her with stiflement. Like Sartre's Roquentin, she is unsure whether this nausea is in herself, or in things about her. She does not give in to it, but resists valiantly. As in her essay, normality is defamiliarized, stripped of its reassuring gloss. Tournier's version of Sartre is a perversion (in his own, nonpejorative sense). In *La Nausée*, the lone-wolf hero undergoes a series of shocks that induce nausea. Instead of the orderliness and meaningfulness he would prefer to find in the physical universe and in human affairs, he experiences in a terminal way, for he has had earlier inklings, the gratuitousness of existence. He rejects suicide as a tenable response, for that would be merely an additional absurd gesture. His retaliation against what causes his nausea, which becomes synonymous with truth, takes the dubious form of harking back to a jazz tune, and projecting a book. He is himself aware of the bad faith involved in such an enterprise of imposing artistic order on the disorder of existence.

For her part, Mélanie has no such hunger for being. Her nausea swamps her at moments when we should say that "l'être *est* le néant." As in all his borrowings, Tournier twists and capitalizes. Similarly, when Mélanie looks through variously colored windowpanes at the garden, Tournier no doubt had in mind the devil's mirror in Hans Christian Andersen's *The Snow Queen*.[5] When it shatters, some fragments become windowpanes, and deforming lenses which invert the appearance and value of all things. The ones Mélanie peers through do not deform, either rosily or blackly. The transformations run the gamut from the horrible to the lovely. The one color lacking is gray—the color of ashy boredom. What she deduces from these optical experiments is that anything can be viewed differently. Such relativity hardly shakes the earth, but she is still young, and is clearly a creature who will push everything to its limits.

When we consider nausea, we think of intake: too much or the wrong kind. Tournier never hints that Mélanie gets sick of people or of herself. It is out there that the problem lies, in things. Hence the stress from the start on sensation and observation. In Mélanie's case, it is foods most readily associated with childhood which provoke her physical nausea: cream, butter, jam. These are all soft, greasy, sticky, and signify a mass or trap to sink into (cf. "le visqueux" in Sartre). The tastes that delight and energize her include green apples, vinegar and pepper: all acid and sharp. As for drinks, milk is bad, lemonade good. She has had to give up her favorite mustard sandwiches, as they caused a riot at school breaks.

Tournier perseveres with his catalogue. He is trying to conjugate her nausea, as a means to making her strange obsessions more comprehensible to the reader, who is possibly jibbing at the idea of a young girl fixated on nausea, nothingness, and death. And so, in terms of weather, Mélanie dislikes hot, lazy afternoons, and prefers cold, dry, bright weather. Summer sun encourages passivity; sunbathing enacts a rape of her supine body. Her tastes go to the bracing. To this end, she gladly embraces both laughter and sobs, which equally shake the frame, and set up distance and control—the very antithesis of docility.

Sobbing and laughter figure strongly in her earlier exposure to death, that of her mother. Her previous experience, of dead animals, had produced disgust at rotting carrion, whereas bleached skeletons, bodies reduced to their essential structure, seem to embody "la bonne mort." Tournier makes little of Mélanie's father's lack of interest in his daughter, who got over her very real grief at her mother's death when she was twelve by picturing her body in the grave as picked clean. Mélanie had killed off a grandmother in her story. Is this a displacement to conceal a wound? Or a more positive option? Tournier has declared: "Les oeuvres sont les fruits du désert et ne s'épanouissent que dans l'aridité" (VP, p. 295). He tells an approving story of a corpse transported across the Sahara, becoming progressively lighter and mummified: "C'est beau, un pays où un cadavre ne pourrit pas."[6] There could be, in his mind, a connection between the clear lines of philosophical systems and the picked bones of a skeleton: the reduction to an essence, or at least a framework. Despite his contrary taste for sumptuousness, Tournier returns often to desiccation or sublimation, as in the anecdote of the blasé socialite, Antoine Bibesco, visiting the plush house of a friend: "Oui d'accord, mais pourquoi pas plutôt rien?" (VP, p. 204). This is Mélanie's priceless question.

It might seem that the mother's death plays a traumatic role comparable to that of the adored sister, Drusilla, in Camus's *Caligula*.[7] Mélanie's envisioning of her mother's stark corpse enables her to "sob with laughter," and to feel "délivrée du poids de l'existence" (p. 181). For such a temperament, mortality renders all human endeavor futile. As death always wins in the end, dying properly seems a more logical goal than living properly. If she cannot be her own cause or origin, she wants to be in charge of her end: "Mine own executioner," as in Donne's *Devotions*. Living is living towards death. Tournier, in many ways a childlike optimist, must have known the temptation to think along these branch lines, to entertain the possibility of welcoming, even hastening, death: "Les hommes du oui imaginent difficilement le monde gris et haineux du non" (*VV*, p. 228). Did the yea-saying author have to wrench his mind in order to rehearse Mélanie's option, which is, however, not gray nor full of hatred (like Caligula), but as orectic towards nothingness as bulimics towards fullness? "La Jeune Fille et la mort" is Tournier's purest fiction.

It has its own impulsion. Even Sartre's *La Nausée* is only an adjunct, not a kick start. Similarly, in the area of intertextuality, Tournier diverges from the burden of Schubert's song, "Death and the Maiden" (based on a poem by Matthias Claudius, about sleeping softly in the arms of death), where the girl initially resists the approaches of Death, protesting that she is too young to die. Death sweet-talks her, explaining that she has nothing to fear. For her part, Mélanie needs no persuading to open herself up to dying. On similar lines to the song, the painting "Death and the Young Woman" by Nicholas Manuel "Deutsch" shows a dirty old man feeling up his prey. It is not entirely clear that she is thwarting him, for she appears to pull his head near hers and to guide his hand to the target area. Tournier presumably wishes to break away from the long tradition of the *danse macabre,* though Mélanie certainly knows the joys of *delectatio morosa*. As for intratextuality, another Schubert song (based on Goethe's poem "Der Erl-König") reveals death as a ravisher-before-time (see *Le Roi des aulnes*). One tradition, that of the *Ars moriendi,* does seem to be revived in Mélanie's hope for "une bonne mort."

Though most of the time Tournier makes Mélanie a likeable creature, on occasion and allowing for the inner logic of her desires, he introduces bleaker perspectives. For instance, at the time of the 1962 Cuban missile crisis when a third world war seemed imminent, Mélanie, quite logically, nurses genocidal dreams. There is always a temptation to generalize from an idiosyncratic case, as Tournier does with Abel Tiffauges or Gilles de Rais. Here, if death rules, why not envisage the massacre of millions? Mélanie soon learns, however, that history, like philosophy later, will not provide any recipe solution for her dilemmas.

Neither will sex, to which she is initiated brutally in the fuel cellar by a delivery boy, Etienne. The rape reads close to attempted murder. Mélanie is both repelled and attracted as her virgin body is assaulted in the dirty room (the white/black motif in another gauzy disguise). In fact, she follows up the rape by visiting Etienne in the wood mill where he works. The savage initiation seems not to have been psychically scarring, probably because of the near-death element in it. The sawdust lying about is an unnoticed foretaste of the story's ending, for it was traditionally used to soak up the blood of the guillotined. It comes, moreover, from tree trunks; and, after decapitation, all that is left of bodies is the trunk. It is at this juncture that Mélanie commissions an elaborate but unspecified machine from a master craftsman. It will be a long job, and the reader probably forgets about this order until the last pages. It is a kind of plant that will flower later.

Mélanie's sexual relationship and sweet nothings with Etienne, satisfying in themselves, continue, but are in no way proof against the death obsession. Tournier writes elsewhere: "La vie a partie liée avec la mort, et la psychanalyse a tort de prétendre opposer Eros et Thanatos comme deux pulsions diamétralement opposées" (CS, p. 173). For Tournier, Freud helps to provide terms for discussion, but no conclusive answers. When Etienne offloads her, Mélanie sinks back again into her *ennui*, from he has been a distraction only. *Ennui* has a long history in the Romantic tradition, although it is difficult to fit Mélanie into this line, as into any other. For Tournier, *ennui* attacks the young especially: "Il y a une lumière glauque d'aquarium tombant sur toutes choses d'un ciel uniformément voilé, et finalement une clameur silencieuse qui brame le désespoir d'exister" (CS, p. 39). He offers as reasons the lack of rootedness, the availability of the young. Mélanie's brief dreams of holocausts derive from Tournier's: "En 1938, 39, 40, j'avais treize, quatorze, quinze ans. Je me souviens de la ferveur avec laquelle je priais pour qu'une guerre éclatât et jetât cul par-dessus tête la société de cloportes où j'agonisais" (CS, p. 40). In comparison, adults are more preoccupied, but far less intense (ibid.). Mélanie has only loose connections with the youthful Tournier, for she bears her fellows no ill will.

Where Mélanie differs from her author or most people is that she decides the solution lies in her own hands. She attaches a rope to a ceiling beam and, like God on the seventh day of creation, she admires her handiwork. Suicide, of course, can be seen as the ultimate gauntlet thrown down before God, or our body (I will die when I decide, not you). The simple act of setting up an exit suddenly gives her life a density it had largely lacked before. She has in effect stepped from the conveyor belt to the self-chosen path. To capture Mélanie's newfound direction, Tournier again resorts to oxymoron. She experiences *un bonheur patibulaire* (p. 187), gallows gaiety, *Galgenfreude* rather than mere passing *Galgenhumor*.

After a sexual liaison, ordinary practicing friendship diverts Mélanie for a spell from her new focus, when her friend Jacqueline asks her to live with her for a few weeks. Apart from her obsession, Mélanie is truly unremarkable, a perfectly decent being, who willingly helps Jacqueline to teach underachieving children. If her fixation is monstrous, she herself is a sympathetic monster. This period is again a truce. Jacqueline's fiancé is in the CRS, a potential death-dealer, as is made plain by his bulky service pistol. Through no fault of her own, Mélanie gets involved in the engaged couple's tiff, and indeed withdraws tactfully from the fraught scene. She is fully prepared for others to be orthodoxly happy. The glimpse of that revolver stays with her, a bulgingly phallic symbol, although it is rather its destructive potentiality that seduces her into stealing it.

Her first stab at suicide is a fiasco. The gun goes off harmlessly while she is trying to find out how it works. She is unsure whether to be relieved or sorry to survive: a wobble in volition that helps to keep her believable. She is typical only of herself. She is simply or complexly a human being with an urge to become an ex-human being. In the woods where she missed her target, she meets a man collecting mushrooms. This encounter opens up more possibilities (death is an eye-opener): self-poisoning. If the reader has not already begun to feel this, her single-minded efforts to do herself in start to become serio-comic here, joco-serious.[8] She has a curiosity about death. She is always ready to learn—about sex, mushrooms, fearsome machines—even if she disbelieves in the lessons of history. For his part, that mushroom expert can flirt safely with death. Mélanie is no tease; she is in earnest (cf. Elizabeth Barrett

Browning: "We shape a figure of our fantasy, / Call nothing something, and run after it").⁹

The sexual motif recurs when Mélanie gets hold of some phallic-shaped lethal fungi. This third possible way out enables Tournier to go through, in willfuly excruciating detail, the various symbolic values of rope, gun and poisonous mushroom, all of which she lays out with the reverence of a sacristan. The pistol, of course, is blatantly erotic, and reminds Mélanie of the undeniable pleasures she had with Etienne. Sex and death, as in the "little death" of Elizabethan orgasm, have been traditional bedmates.¹⁰ Beyond such local thrills, all three instruments of suicide seem to open different doors on to the unknown, as if death itself were the afterlife. The plethora of available methods suggests that Mélanie's nausea surfaces not from a lack of meaning, but from a surfeit.¹¹

In his ebullient catalogue, Tournier proposes that mushrooms betoken a giant stomach and all the basic existential activities associated with it: digestion, sex and evacuation. Mélanie imagines dying from mushroom poisoning as an initiation ceremony. It would be like being born in reverse, a return to a primeval (not an identifiably maternal) womb. The pistol, for its share, evokes Hell: flames, noise, acrid stench. The third key to the door of the unknown, the rope, and the chair to take off from, represent Nature, trees and plants. If she chose this route, she could feel part of the landscape. In this section, as well as intentionally parodying experts like the mycologist-philosopher Coquebin, Tournier pastiches himself in this symbolic disquisition. Would Mélanie, without his ventriloquism, be up to articulating such finesses? Whether or not, she clearly wants what, in Starobinski's account, Montaigne desired: "La mort idéale, pour Montaigne, est une mort agie, une 'mort dirigée' (comme nous parlons d'accouchement dirigé) où la conscience s'applique étroitement à l'événement instantané qui se produit dans la profondeur du corps."¹²

To Mélanie's options Tournier opposes the very different views of the pedant, M. Coquebin (i.e., greenhorn). The décor of his room, with its plaster saints, indicates religiosity, and indeed a leading Catholic saint, Theresa, object of a particularly sentimental cult, lived once in the next street. When Mélanie looks quietly consternated at such talk—she entirely lacks mystical velleities—he swiftly changes to another hobbyhorse, philosophy. Immediately he runs up against her refusal to argue, to justify herself, or to proselytise. She is uninterested in the high-flown shoptalk of philosophy. Tournier is not alone, however, in thinking that "l'enfant est spontanément philosophe, métaphysicien même."[13] The frontispiece of *Le Vent Paraclet* shows Franz von Lenbach's shepherd-boy daydreaming on his back. Tournier glosses: "Il scrute le vide lumineux. Il se laisse basculer dans ce gouffre d'azur... C'est sa façon à lui de faire de la métaphysique." When Mélanie tells Coquebin without affectation the story of her life so far, he at once intellectualizes it and slots it into scholastic traditions.[14]

When Mélanie relates her experiment with the colored windowpanes, he knee-jerkily, by professional or amateur deformation, cites Kant's aesthetic theories. The more she tells, the more convinced he grows that she has, quite independently, reached the same conclusions as the two main philosophical currents over the ages. One stems from Parmenides—a philosophy emphasizing the static, unchanging nature of being. Mélanie's fixation on death and mummified corpses could lodge here. The second wells from Heraclitus, the philosopher of flux; and the rest of Mélanie's discrete life incidents might tag along here. The opposition is also that of Cain and Abel, the sedentary and the nomad. But Mélanie hankers neither to roam nor to settle down. Such polarities leave her untouched. As he expatiates, Coquebin eventually realizes that his interlocutor is far more preoccupied by a single red hair jutting out of a mole on his cheek than by his pedantic lecture. She is taken with concrete particulars, not structures and systems. As such, she is the antithesis of Tournier himself at her age, who worshipped only "le système avec son insurpassable cohérence, ... cause de tout, effet de rien" (*VP*, p. 157); and who looks back with fond amusement at "ces coups de poing tambourinant mes pectoraux de petit Tarzan métaphysicien" (*VP*, p. 180). Mélanie is no more cut out to be a willful nonconformist than a conformist. She is a nonesuch, neither etched black and white, nor dully gray.

Feminists might detect in this portrait of the girl an ancient stereotype: women, no matter how perceptive, seen as relying on intuition rather than reasoning powers. Yet we have seen how logical she is, and male rationalism as embodied or disembodied in Coquebin is lampooned. When she stops visiting him, she again becomes a prey to *ennui*. She is getting nowhere fast. The crunch is clearly coming. She cannot postpone forever a decision, accumulating instruments of death that she puts to no use. She is getting bored with her *ennui*. And so she opts for a deadline. This coincides with the feast day of St. Theresa, who died young herself, after likewise losing her mother at an early age. At fourteen, she was fascinated (like Mélanie with Damiens) by the murderer Pranzini. Her lively autobiography, *The Story of a Soul*, aimed to show that spiritual perfection could be achieved through childlike humility. Mélanie is not ostentatiously humble, but what arrogance she has is not targeted at others. It is the genuine arrogance of somebody who knows very definitely what she wants. She wants out. She will stop at nothing to have her way.

The decision reached, Mélanie is elated. She sees death as a process of transfiguration—another instance of Tournier's recycling of Christian tenets to unorthodox ends. Though she has fixed the deadline, we do not know which method she has chosen. Admittedly, she returns to her woodland cottage, where the rope waits, but she could equally well use the gun or the poisonous fungi fittingly there. Principally, she is seeking seclusion, having no desire to appall others. Two days before the appointed day, a van delivers the machine commissioned long before. Tournier uses the colloquial, revolutionary term, *la veuve* (an example of gallows humour).

Wittgenstein famously said: "What we cannot talk about we must pass over in silence,"[15] but the philosopher who declared that a wholly serious treatise consisting entirely of jokes was conceivable might well have allowed for mute, inner quaking.[16] There is a possible connection between "le rire blanc" and the narrative blank which Tournier tries to circumscribe thus:

> Absolu. Un concept qui pour exprimer le comble de la positivité emprunte une tournure négative. Ab-solu, qui n'a pas de lien, sans rapport, non relatif. Or tout ce que nous sommes, tout ce que nous connaissons est tellement relié-à, c'est-à-dire relatif, que le contraire devient pour nous inexprimable. A la limite, comme certains écrivains religieux qui se refusent à écrire le mot Dieu, laisser un blanc à la place d'absolu.[17]

The narrative blank, or blackout, in "La Jeune Fille et la mort," like the elision of the Fall in "La Famille Adam," or the children-only performance in "Que ma joie demeure," digs a hole, introduces nothingness. The narrative switches from the arrival of *la veuve* to a doctor who has just examined Mélanie's corpse. He is tempted to a paradox, which is also an everyday idiom: she has died laughing. Ever the roguish pedant, Tournier then further bifurcates into a physiological account of the phenomenon of laughter. Anyone who has ever read the deathless prose of laboratory tests on a sense of humor will cheer Tournier's mockery. Just as Coquebin's potted history of metaphysical speculation got us nowhere towards understanding Mélanie's idiosyncratic version, so the doctor's borrowed dissection of laughter leaves untouched her special brand: cosmic hilarity. When he was a student, it was the concrete, not the abstract, aspects of philosophy that appealed to Tournier; and humor always returns or anchors us in the concrete. From the poetic materialist Bachelard especially he claims to have learned that the nearer you get to the ultimate questions (e.g., The Meaning of Life), the likelier you are to be convulsed with laughter (see *VP*, pp. 152–53). Levity and gravity coexist, cooperate.

For his contribution to the debate, Coquebin quotes the well-publicized comic theory of Bergson: comedy results when something mechanical is encrusted on the living; when, for example, people start behaving like automata. Bergson's *Le Rire* is essentially concerned with cliché, existential stereotypes. Bergson's dogmatic notions seem at home in the vicinity of the guillotine. They smack of the policeman: killjoy and punitive, a method of social correction and of imposing uniformity. Given Tournier's and Mélanie's individualism, such a comic ideology is itself risible. Arthur Koestler performed a perfect demolition of Bergson's over-influential hypothesis:

> If automatic repetitiveness in human behaviour were a necessary and sufficient condition of the comic, there would be no more amusing spectacle than an epileptic fit. If "we laugh each time a person gives us the impression of being a thing," there would be nothing more funny than a corpse.[18]

If, as suggested earlier, Mélanie's single-mindedness is in part comic, it still involves mind, will, and imagination: she is no Bergsonian robot. Elsewhere, Tournier judges Bergson's theory adequate, but only for "le rire de société" (*VP*, p. 197). "White" or

"cosmic" laughter (i.e., not sick or black, but coolly aristocratic) cuts far wider and deeper:

> Le cosmique et le comique. Ces deux mots qui paraissent faits pour être rapprochés . . . Il y a un comique cosmique: celui qui accompagne l'émergence de l'absolu au milieu du tissu de relativités où nous vivons. C'est le rire de Dieu. Car nous nous dissimulons le néant qui nous entoure, mais il perce parfois la toile peinte de notre vie (*VP*, p. 198)

Death makes strange.

As so often, Tournier calls in henchmen. Nietzsche, whose whole work "est parcourue par un friselis de drôlerie qui sape les racines mêmes de l'être" (*VP*, p. 200). Tournier himself is not innocent of the "persiflage métaphysique" he finds in Thomas Mann, although he concedes that the account in *The Magic Mountain* of a patient tickled by unearthly laughter while undergoing the unspeakable agony of a pneumothorax is exactly what he means by "le rire blanc" (*VP*, pp. 202–3). In that same novel, Hans Castorp's mother "meurt tout simplement en riant, meurt de rire à la lettre, tuée par l'inénarrable drôlerie de la condition humaine."[19]

In contrast with the doctor or Coquebin, Mélanie's friend Jacqueline, an ordinary mortal, aspires to no sophisticated interpretation, and offers a novelettish version of the death. Consumed with passion for the riot-squaddy, Mélanie has sacrificed herself for her friend's happiness. Only the old craftsman, Sureau, does not waste words trying to read the event. He may be a stand-in for Tournier, who fondly describes himself as an artisan, who works long-windedly, and who has produced in his story a beautiful machine of destruction for his young heroine. Nobody in the story, starting with the teacher on the first page, has even begun to understand Mélanie. She nonplusses experts and laypersons alike. Her death's-head grin recalls that of the Cheshire cat. She dies, *aenigma intactum*.

Tournier winks to Alphonse Allais, one of the cream of French humorists, coiner of the epithet, when he has Mélanie send out "un faire-part anthume" (p. 201), which summons all who knew her, but is timed so that they will get to her forest hut too late to dissuade her. Foreign aid would be over her dead body. Her suicide note is no cry for help. The three weapons in her arsenal stand unused. She has died, in purely medical terms, of a massive heart

attack (cf. "Les attaques cérébrales, si commodes pour ménager le coup de théâtre qui débarrasse l'auteur d'un personnage devenu inutile, reculent devant l'infarctus de myocarde plus moderne, plus business, plus noble aussi parce que touchant le coeur" (VV, p. 326). Her dead face retains a smile. Twisting congealed syntagms as so often, Tournier switches "la joie de vivre" to "la joie de ne pas vivre."[20]

To add to the lexical stock-pot, I would offer "nihility": the opposite of plenitude; "neminity": the opposite of egoistic pride, the urge to be no one; and "nusquamity": the opposite of ubiquity, the urge to be nowhere. Such neologisms imply that negatives are real (to nill countervails to will), and have to bear thinking about.[21] They clear the way for the indescribable. Mélanie's essay, about a nonevent, represents Tournier's attempt in this story as a whole to evoke the positive desire to be nothing, the ambition to be dead. Saying "no" has its own reasons, its own consistency. Whereas death is traditionally associated with terminal coldness, repeated images of warmth accompany Mélanie's explorations (pp. 186, 193). Christian orthodoxy, of course, highlights Satan, the rebel angel who set up shop in rivalry with God (cf. Tournier's self-estimate), as the spirit who nay-says. A cipher is a letter, and a code, as well as zero. "Giotto's O" was legendarily taken to represent artistic perfection. Queneau opined mildly: "Rien. Rien offre des avantages," and his hero Jacques "s'efforce de se tarir, de se désencombrer, de s'évider. Il dégorge son trop-plein de moi . . . Il se dépeuple."[22] Piling on thick seems inextricably tied with evacuation, excess with lessness. Mélanie is another exponent of nontology.[23]

When someone in the cottage asks what is the large object wrapped in black linen, old Sureau unveils the guillotine, not as if it were a mature widow, *la veuve,* but rather as if it were a young bride he is gently undressing. It is a work of art. It embodies everything that Mélanie always valued: it is clean, cold, a perfect machine for the task in hand. It is also, divertingly, heavily decorated and somewhat ridiculous with its hodgepodge of styles: ancient Greek, late eighteenth-century. Coquebin identifies this composite, neoclassical, anti-rococo style as Louis XV1—the reigning monarch guillotined in 1793 (cf. the earlier list of famous figures executed). The ancestor of the French guillotine was the Maiden (also known as the Widow), used in Scotland in the sixteenth and seventeenth centuries for criminals. Maiden here means first, as in maiden voyage. Mélanie wants to *handsel* death, to inaugurate it with pleasure. She wants to do herself in in style. In another text, Tournier recounts the anecdote of a village carpenter who built a beautiful guillotine, placed his head in the *lunette,* and pressed the switch:

> Il faudrait réserver une place parmi les causes du suicide à la force de persuasion qui émane d'un instrument de mort du seul fait de sa perfection technique ou artistique. Pas plus qu'on ne peut se retenir de goûter à certains gâteaux ou de faire l'amour avec certains corps, on ne saurait refuser à certains poignards, à certains pistolets, l'acte qu'ils appellent de toute leur admirable forme. (CS, p. 173)

This instrumental persuasion presumably acts like the chasm breeding vertigo and the urge to jump in acrophobics. Dr. Louis Guillotin's machine, when first proposed, was greeted with much hilarity. Ambrose Bierce defined the guillotine as "a machine which makes a Frenchman shrug his shoulders with good reason."[24]

Whether or not Mélanie intended to use the guillotine, this object, blackly comic, has helped her to die laughing. For who needs a fabulous mechanism when an inside job, the heart attack, suffices? An infarctus round the time you choose is the ultimate form of do-it-yourself. Viewing the guillotine in all its sinister glory, a machine that symbolizes how most people probably think of death: a violent intrusion, which cuts us off in our prime, gives Mélanie the supreme occasion for active derision. "Une mort parfaite doit ressembler à la vie qu'elle couronne comme son ultime achèvement" (CS, p. 172). *Donnant donnant,* giff gaff, fair's fair. She dies laughing, and no mistake. From what we know of her, her final act would have been to laugh out quiet.

From another angle, typified by Robert Burns's "The best-laid schemes o' mice an' men / Gang aft agley," no one can successfully prepare for death; it will always catch us on the hop, and thus make us laugh the other side of our faces. The heart attack just happened, out of the blue: an ambush. Even then, Mélanie has still been able to die laughing, at herself and her own overpreparedness for death, because a cosmic sense of humor enables you to distance yourself and to find everything, even your own precious self, risible. No emperor has any clothes. This is clearly the rarest, the most rarefied, kind of humor. It seems inevitable for those tempted to think along such lines to conceive of mocking laughter, *dérision*. Whatever power it is that made an absurd world seems to be enjoying a good laugh at our expense. If, however, you are lucidly alive to the situation, as Mélanie intuitively is, you can join in the divine or diabolical joke. Wittingly or dimly, Tournier derides his own propensity for elaborate systems, and recognizes that master planners can always be outsmarted. In Coquebin, Tournier skits his own recurrent pretension of using philosophic categories to try to corral life's mysteries.

Tournier offers no criticism of Mélanie (unlike Véronique, Lucien, Pierre). Her excess, her longing for negation, come across as entirely positive, just as her essay on death was highly animated. "Certaines personnes m'ont dit que Mélanie c'était Amandine devenue grande, ce n'est pas une mauvaise interprétation."[25] We leave Amandine on the trembling threshold of teenage fecundity. Maybe what Mélanie is escaping is, amongst other things, her female *fatum*. She lacks maternal vocation, and Tournier does not encourage us to think that she wants to rejoin her mother. Mélanie, like other Tournier activists, experiences *amor fati*, defined as "la lente métamorphose du destin en destinée . . . d'un mécanisme obscur et coercitif en l'élan unanime et chaleureux d'un être vers son accomplissement" (*VP*, p. 242). Mélanie, however, is unusual in the panoply of heroes and heroines, in not seeking to generalize her obsession, nor even to let it affect others. Those things that human beings normally rely on to fill out their lives—love, friendship, ambition—have not been enough to anchor her. For Tournier, the mass of mankind are "suradaptés," living like fish in water, and not questioning their environment nor their mental climate. Society is a vast cliché factory, "une pensée stéréotypée," from which few withdraw their labor (*VV*, p. 51).

Perhaps she goes on to enjoy exalted company. For Nietzsche, the old gods laughed themselves to death, and Zarathustra added: "Truly it will be the death of me, to choke with laughter."[26] Like Novalis after the death of his adored Sophie or Kleist in his suicide pact with his beloved, the good die young: "Les vies les meilleures ne connaissent pas de phase adulte" (*VP*, p. 290). Death is unmistakably the last chance for initiation, as contrasted with mere sufferance. Tournier favors initiation stories over *Bildungsromane*. The latter afford *atterrissage*, whereas "l'initiation est un excellent décollage."²⁷ *Décollage:* unsticking (from the viscous here-and-now) and, more anciently, decapitation. Mélanie wants to initiate herself; her desire to die does without intervention by others. Above all, initiation is not confrontation nor assimilation, but transcendence.²⁸ Neither does Mélanie's effort chime in with the classic Existentialist angst about human mortality. Death does not spoil all but gives added spice, point, and vitality. Mélanie's living-towards-death echoes the Heideggerian idea *(Sein zum Tode)* which Sartre contradicts so fiercely in "Le Mur." Mélanie refuses Sisyphus' stoic, stick-at-it option. Even if Camus enjoins us to imagine his hero, in his living death, happy, we are not invited to picture him splitting his sides.

To counter the quotations opening this study, I bring in Aldous Huxley: "Can you really say something about nothing?"²⁹ Tournier has done his damnedest to do so, by thinking against himself more than usual, against his own majority instincts. That he impersonates Mélanie so persuasively is a sign that he is a truly polymorphous-perverse writer, and that she represents a temptation, a Valéry-type "mauvaise pensée" for her creator, a reverse-thrust of his mental mechanism. The fact remains that Tournier still speaks for her *ennui;* he dictates it, to her and to readers. Apart from inability, this results from his view of what is "un conte": "Une nouvelle hantée. Hantée par une signification fantomatique qui nous touche, nous enrichit, mais ne nous éclaire pas" (*VV*, p. 40). As Davis suggests, "Tournier's texts engage the reader in the quest for understanding, but never arrive at a fully intelligible conclusion."³⁰ Like Mélanie's essay, Tournier has made something out of nothing, Mélanie's desire to be nothing.

12
The Fetish of Not Seeing: "Le Coq de bruyère"

This story, unusually for Tournier, focused on conventional society and its mores, concerns a man and his wife who live according to supposedly inflexible codes of belief and conduct, which both of them violate in differing ways. It starts with a fencing match, and indeed for much of its duration the marital duo fight a kind of duel.

The baron, an army colonel, is an oxymoron, *senex juvenis*, "une belle et juvénile soixantaine" (*CB*, p. 205). This sprightly victor will be vanquished. Not precisely a case of mutton dressed as lamb, he is, in another oxymoronic twist, "un vieillard prodige" (p. 206). He is cock of the walk, *un coq de bruyère*.[1] In his values and habits, he is a classical French cavalry officer, devoted to socializing, womanizing, fencing, and riding. He is known for joking that he prefers horses to women. His favorite mount, a mare, is called Fleurette. Tournier puns unashamedly on this name: *se battre au fleuret* (foil fencing); *conter fleurette* (to tell a woman sweet nothings). The colonel's different pursuits overlap. Women are prey to be hunted, or horses to be broken and ridden. So little is truly left to chance in Tournier's fictional universe, or chance is so often converted to inevitability, that even puns, those phonic fortuities, are pressed into service with increasing pointedness as this story progresses. As the baron has few inner resources—his whole energy is directed outwards—he experiences periodic *ennui*, though of a kind less richly complex than that of Mélanie in "La Jeune Fille et la mort." He will have one last fling, or spring, before his years, and indeed his whole lifestyle, catch up with him.

We first encounter his wife, older than he and much more given to an orderly life, in conversation with her confessor, a scene which gives Tournier the opportunity for satirical pastiche. The abbé waxes naively lyrical about nature in springtime. In contrast, the baroness displays a rough-tongued aristocratic cynicism about the chances of anything or anyone, including children, ever being pure. When they discuss the need for a new serving girl, the baroness is under no illusion about the risks involved, given her husband's taste for seducing social inferiors; there have been previous scandals. She is, at this stage, open-eyed.

As the colonel prepares to go off hunting, his wife warns him that one of these days he will break his neck and she will end up pushing him around in a wheelchair. Which is what indeed will happen, except that a failed love affair will be the equivalent of his falling off a horse. Sparring, as they generally do, they exchange jibes about the paucity of their sexual relations. The colonel justifies his preference for other women's beds: "Vous n'êtes pas *une* femme, vous êtes *ma* femme" (p. 216). This polarity of woman and wife possibly reflects Tournier's own habitual equating of marriage with legalized boredom. He manages the marriage-bed gripes with sardonic wit. It suits the baron to recall his sainted mother's words when they went to her for a blessing on their marriage. She instructed the future wife to see to his every need, which he evidently interprets as indulging his every whim.

Selecting candidates for the maid's post is the next duel. The baroness would prefer the unlikely combination of a woman who would look pleasant in her eyes but not in her husband's (and eyes is the key word here, as throughout the story). The perfect appointee of the colonel would be young, petite, shapely, and docile. A kind of harem slave is what he has in mind, or on the brain.[2] Coincidentally, the film on at the local cinema is *Bluebeard,* the notorious tyrant over women. Roguishly male again, the baron puns on the set phrase *bonne à tout faire* (maid of all work, or a woman ready to do anything for a man) and extends it: "délicieuse à tout faire . . . exquise à tout faire" (p. 221). He wants his dream creature, inspired by the filmstar Cécile Aubry, to be flirtatious, slightly hard to get, but vanquishable: the chase must pay off. Such fond visualizations are comically deflated when he finds that the baroness's actual choice, Eugénie, is fifty, with the beginnings of a moustache and the build of a garbageman. The wife has scored a significant point.

12: THE FETISH OF NOT SEEING: "LE COQ DE BRUYÈRE"

Bulky as a wardrobe herself, Eugénie easily shifts the heaviest furniture, and farce intrudes when one day she sends the colonel flying as she is walking backward, humping a chest of drawers. In league with her mistress, she quickly imposes imperious female order on the house in the great ritual of spring cleaning. Though the baroness claims not to be a fanatic of cleanliness like her grandmother, who compelled her maid to pick out fluff from between floorboards with a pin, she clearly enjoys the power involved in the big cleanout. When she and Eugénie unearth the colonel's collection of pornographic magazines, Tournier captures very astutely the complicity between the two ageing women, who agree what filthy pigs men are, while at the same time preserving the social niceties: Eugénie must be less candidly censorious than her mistress.

Reminiscing about her girlhood at a convent school, the baroness recalls that, at bath time, the girls had to wear a coarse, heavy cape under which they got undressed, washed, dried, and dressed again. Tournier is inventing nothing here, since such a practice was common in some nineteenth-century homes. It obviously stems from a fear of awakening sexuality or indeed of any interest in one's own body. The convent sisters, with prettifying euphemism, would explain that the guardian angel of each girl was a beautiful, bashful, chaste young man, who needed to be spared troubling glimpses of young female bodies. Though up to now the baroness has seemed fairly hard-bitten, here she betrays a tenderly romantic soul. She confesses that her ideal man (in contrast with her husband's dream woman) is precisely that pure young guardian angel. This ideal is not, despite appearances, sexless; indeed, her ejaculations on seeing her husband's erotica were already ambivalent.

Spring is traditionally the season of climatic and corporeal disorder and overspill. In this story, the catalyst for the drama is Eugénie's niece, Mariette, who stands in when her aunt has to return home for a spell on family business. Mariette is a Cécile Aubry lookalike. Overjoyed at this last chance of rebecoming the twenty-year-old lieutenant he once was, the colonel begins to remodel her to his tastes, sending her to a beautician in order to superimpose sophistication on to the rougher charms of the country girl.[3] When he decides to set Mariette up in her own flat in town, he discloses the absurd aspect of his code of honor, for he has sullied the family home before. He is in fact upholding a stereotype (the "bit on the side"), though he persuades himself that Mariette is a special case, his last chance of extra-conjugal bliss. He wants to go out in a blaze of glory.

When the baroness finds out about the love nest, Tournier records the sexist French convention which favors the sinning male against the wronged wife. Consulting her father confessor, she hears the sermon of forgiveness, and the heavily loaded advice: "Fermez les yeux" (p. 234). On the conscious level, she is too proud to obey, but some deeper level of her being acts on the counsel. She begins to lose her sight. Throughout the story, Tournier cleverly switches our sympathies from one partner to the other. One day the baron discovers his wife reading, in Braille. The shock and his sense of honor oblige him to say good-bye to Mariette. Nobly, for weeks, he keeps his word, tending his wife devotedly. He behaves in an exemplary, edifying fashion. Tournier is never more suspicious of anyone or anything than when they are conventionally edifying. His own didactic urges are deep-rooted, but almost entirely subversive.

When her sight begins to return, she and the abbé soon realize that, far from being a miracle, it is a seriously mixed blessing, or even a poisoned gift. In a curious way, this "happy event" is more scandalous than her husband's illicit affair. She will in fact have to hide her regained sight, or she will lose him again, for he will conclude that she has been merely pretending to be blind. The good abbé approves of her subterfuge. Her intentions are virtuous (saving a marriage), even if her conduct (deceit) is sinful—a splendidly jesuitical compromise. She may piously hope to undeceive her husband gradually, but truth has little fondness for being doled out. At the traditional bourgeois ceremony of the Sunday promenade in town, the colonel sees Mariette on the arm of a young man. This hurts him enough but, when he realizes that his supposedly blind wife is smiling, he feels cuckolded twice over.

He rushes in anger to Paris in order to consult a specialist in psychosomatic medicine. Like any explanatory grille which straddles boundaries, psychosomatic theory must have some appeal for Tournier. Although the whole area is notoriously tricky and so difficult to prove or disprove, most psychologists would concede at least a likelihood of reality in the realm of autosuggested illness. Laypeople themselves know full well that mind and body interre-

12: THE FETISH OF NOT SEEING: "LE COQ DE BRUYÈRE"

late in numerous flummoxing ways. As a bluff military man, the colonel has little patience for fancy talk, and he fully expects the doctor to lisp effeminately. This doctor has found absolutely nothing wrong physically with the baroness. Her blindness was self-induced.[4] He goes on to give a brief survey of Freud's principal psychoanalytical divisions: the ego, the id, and the superego. The colonel transmutes this jargon into military terms, and instinctively favors the idea of malingering on the part of his wife.

What is at issue here is the proposal that the baroness has subconsciously willed her blindness, in order to shut her eyes to what she loathed to see: her husband's infidelity. The colonel clearly finds this diagnosis too near the knuckle, as it makes him the cause, the trauma, behind the blindness. He expresses his indignation in a telling pun: "J'étais venu ici avec le soupçon qu'on me menait en bateau. J'ai maintenant la certitude qu'on essaie de m'embarquer sur une galère!" (p. 250). When he confronts his wife, he emphasizes her responsibility for her state. In general, Tournier finds Freudian theory too reductive, yet in this instance it does appear to fit quite well the events of the story. The colonel's rejection in part of the theory reflects more on him than on Freud. Furthermore, a key reason why, for once, Tournier gives an expert a run for his money, is that this area of psychological behavior unites the voluntarism central to his thinking with the sense of overarching fate that houses this willfulness: collaboration, "amor fati."[5]

For his own part willfully ignoring the evidence of another man in Mariette's life, the colonel picks up where he left off. He resumes fencing and riding, once more "le coq de bruyère." He tells all who ask that it is perfect bliss with Mariette. There are certainly moments of climactic joy, though he wonders at times whether they will kill him off. Mariette retains her young lover; the colonel is still being duped. Now he too starts using the fateful phrase "fermer les yeux." One day he finds a scrabbled-up note. It is naive; Mariette can see no moral problem in a three-sided relationship. Meanwhile spring has yielded to summer; the town is devoid of distractions. The baron wanders aimlessly back to his house, which he finds abandoned.

The last page or so is nightmare. As he stands before the vacated house and his own empty existence, he begins to feel nausea, then anguish. Two black silhouettes advance on him, accompanied by the tapping of a white stick. The colonel collapses into the gutter. It is ambiguous whether he has had a stroke, or whether his fall gave him a cerebral hemorrhage. When his wife and Eugénie, the two figures in black, pick him up, he is hemiplegic, his right side paralyzed.

Devotion, Tournier insists often, is repression. "Servir et asservir, aimer et tuer. Cette terrible dialectique est la constante de nombre d'êtres humains vivant le couple à leur façon" (*VP,* p. 125). The pair of women devote themselves utterly to caring for the terminally tethered baron. His wife's code of honor demands this (and she remembers her mother-in-law's injunction). The humor is willfully black when Tournier comments that, what with the baroness blind again and the baron's semiparalysis, they are linked together in an edifying symbol of conjugal fidelity. Our last sight of the couple is on that ritual Sunday promenade. Her eyesight has by now returned, as she no longer has anything to dread, nothing from which to avert her gaze. She pushes the wheelchair which, earlier, she had said awaited her husband if he persisted in taking part in dangerous sports. The old "coq de bruyère" is decrepit, shrunken, melancholy—a cruel parody of what he once had been. One side of his face is locked in a permanent leer. For the last words in the story, Tournier repeats sardonically the colonel's inaccurate description of his liaison with Mariette: "Perfect bliss."

In his active life, the colonel had pursued a largely social role, a male stereotype. No role now remains but that of the recipient of nursing, an inert object. All of the characters in this tale shut their eyes. The abbé, because he always forgives transgressors; the baroness, most centrally; the colonel, to Mariette's faithlessness. "Les Suaires de Véronique" features an erotic fetish of seeing. Here, the baroness closes her eyes to sexuality, though she allows herself a few peeps from under the eyelids.

Altogether, "Le Coq de bruyère" is a more leisurely and relaxed story than most in this collection, partly because its plot strewn with ironies is in several ways reminiscent of nineteenth-century realist stories, such as those of Maupassant. Tournier himself admitted: "Je traite le sujet par défi, pour me prouver que même dans le domaine je peux faire mieux que les spécialistes Maurois, Chardonne."[6] Elsewhere, distinguishing as usual *la nouvelle* from *le conte,* he maintains that a *nouvelle* is marked by "une horizontalité austère [qui] exclut tout au-delà, toute transcendance" (VV, p. 39). Marriage, adultery, deceit, and self-blinding are clearly lacking, for Tournier, in the kind of depth for which he reserves the accolade transcendant. To return his sneer, we might wonder whether there is some connection between bachelorhood, such as Tournier's, and preference for the general(ized). There are certainly no happy couples in his work. His heroes ultimately seek to go beyond the individual. Abel Tiffauges is obsessed with *all* the schoolchildren he photographs so ogrishly, then with all his juvenile charges at the *napola*. Be that as it may, this story has more space, less cramming, more room for details of no especial symbolic significance, such as the fact that the colonel makes his own cartridges for his shotgun.

Just as puns are turns of phrase, so this whole story hinges on a pun: "fermer les yeux." The physical becomes metaphorical, and then physical again, in a changed and more troubling sense. "Fermer les yeux" is what the moribund do, or, on their behalf, their watchers. In *Les Météores,* Paul's sense of psychic bereftness leads to corporeal mutilation. Puns come true; language can create, as well as reflect, reality. There is an evident link here with the realm of the psychosomatic; mind/body, figurative/literal. For Tournier, in general, words have two faces and forked tongues. Puns link up with his leitmotif of "inversion maligne/bénigne," for wordplay deals itself in such inversions; punning and ethical twisting have long been likened to each other. In all this, it is impossible to separate the serious from the ludic, for how can puns be deemed "excruciating," unless they touch some vital nerve?

13

Cain and Abel Revisited: "L'Aire du Muguet"

THIS story has a recognizably contemporary setting: lorries and motorways. It seems more down-to-earth than the other stories. Yet it is Cain and Abel in alternative dress again. Here Pierre, a creature of habit, will suffer from doing an Abel; his break of routine will have lethal consequences. In his stay-at-home mother's eyes, Pierre leads the free life, cruising up and down the A6 between Paris and Lyons.[1] The repeated stress on rituals and habits in the opening pages, however, suggests that the traveller Pierre is, in effect, on rails. He is fated.

As soon as he is reunited each morning with his articulated truck, he feels elated; he takes a childish joy in his "enormous plaything" (*AM*, p. 262).[2] Pierre keeps the windscreen, above all, immaculate, so that the lorry can have a clear conscience, a poetic notion that is developed later. His co-driver, Gaston, is older and more cautious in all things. Though friendly, their relationship involves a good deal of bickering. On the open road, whereas Pierre feels free of home, Gaston takes his protective shell with him, like a snail or tortoise. He prefers home comforts, traditional cooking, comfortable clothes, and is altogether a more maternal figure opposed to the more obviously macho Pierre. In one exchange of disagreements, Gaston reminds his young mate that while he has already been Pierre's age, Pierre cannot be certain he will ever reach Gaston's age: a mild statement that will become sinister only with hindsight. A further implication is that Gaston already possesses what he desires, whereas Pierre still pursues his fulfillment.

Of different generations, they disagree about *connerie* (literally "stupidity," but covering a wide range of pretensions: idealism, talking big, mystification). Gaston had a bellyful of *connerie* in wartime, before Pierre was born. He is sceptical of the younger man's lyricism, centered on the appeal of the open road, which Pierre sees as offering endless, exciting possibilities, even though their many shuttle journeys so far have been marked only by consecrated routine. Pierre utters the fateful words: "L'autoroute, faut y être. Faut en être. Faut pas en sortir" (p. 271). Fate itself, and one of its familiar aspects, romantic love, will be linked with *connerie* in due course. Pierre will be a fool for love.

On one of the regular rest breaks on the A6, "L'Aire du Muguet,"[3] Pierre takes a brief trip away from the concrete jungle of the motorway. Its din fades; he feels at peace and happy as when, years before, he went up to his little sister's cradle. This is a short excursion in time (or out of it) as well as in space. He has a vision of a blonde girl in a pink dress sitting in the grass. They are separated by a fence, which is enough to deter him from speaking to her. On the return trip, she is not there. Significantly, though the field has cows in it, he thinks of her as *la bergère*, as in idyllic love stories. When she appears, she is more truly peasant-like close up than he remembered, though he is just as enchanted. Her name is Marinette, a stock name in poems and songs about country girls. Whereas Pierre, naively, is all for progress (fast roads, fast food), Marinette has suffered from it. A local wood and its lily-of-the-valley have had to be sacrificed for the motorway; and there is no one to takeover her father's farm when he dies. On Pierre's return to the lorry, Gaston raises the question of marriage. His own wife deserted him for a grocer. The home-bird Gaston has paid a price for being constantly away on the road; Cain has become a lonely Abel.

Connerie has comical sides. On one stop, which prepares for the black farce of the finale, Pierre is caught by a highway patrol in the act of climbing the fence into the girl's field. To Gaston, he waxes lyrical and warm, no doubt inspired by the sight of Marinette, about humans and animals in a farmhouse sharing the same living space. As Gaston reminds him, Pierre has never in fact lived like that, so his memories are pure imagination. Tournier frequently lauds such hankerings or nostalgias: life-forms intertwined, work and play cohabiting, the outside brought indoors, the abolition of barriers. Pierre admits he is imagining, but swears such values are in his blood. For all his philosophizing about lorries and the charging onward on the open road, Pierre cannot explain why he looks backward also to peasant forbears. Though nowhere near as wide-ranging as Mélanie Blanchard, Pierre does have a philosophical turn of mind. Tournier is no intellectual snob and readily credits anyone, however educationally unexceptional, with the capacity to articulate complex thoughts.

The next time he sees Marinette and asks her to go dancing with him, she offers to dance there and then, to her transistor, with the fence between them. And so they dance together apart (another oxymoron), as Gaston watches bemused. This scene is linked thematically to the following one, where Pierre picks up on his earlier concern for a spotless windscreen, and marries it to memories of looking in shop windows at Christmastime. There the glass acts as a barrier, saying: do not touch. If you step inside to ask for the goods displayed, they seem less desirable. In motorway terms, the windscreen is the shop window, and the landscape and all it contains the untouchable ideal, best gaped at from a safe distance. Elsewhere, Tournier complains bitterly about "toute notre civilisation faite de vitrines où l'on ne peut 'toucher' qu'avec ses yeux. Cette pseudo-morale du 'bas-les-pattes' vient tout droit de l'Angleterre victorienne" (*VI*, p. 45). The French term "lèche-vitrines" does indeed have a melancholy as well as an exultantly sensuous potentiality. "L'homme d'aujourd'hui se promène muselé et manchot dans un palais de mirages" (*CS*, p. 26). Although Tournier protests this puritanical fear of touching, Pierre will in fact suffer for his hunger to grasp what attracts him.

Tournier at this point uses the affectionate, diminutive form of Pierre's name, Pierrot—the white-faced harlequin, eager for love but so often disappointed. When Gaston perceptively draws the analogy between the passing, rolling landscape and girls, he reveals his variant romantic streak. In their rest periods, Gaston reads a novelette, a desert romance, which inspires in him a comparison between long-distance lorry drivers and Arab nomads. Tournier again affords himself some pastiche,—here of the conventions of popular pulp fiction. Not that he belittles Gaston's tastes. Gaston needs his myths, too, even if they are banal and safely distanced in an exotic neverland. Unlike Pierre, Gaston keeps his dream provender and his daily bread in separate compartments. In addition, Tournier might be hinting: who needs de-

13: CAIN AND ABEL REVISITED: "L'AIRE DU MUGUET"

sert romances, when the A6 in France can provide surprising adventures? The everyday can be filled with the marvelous. From now on, Pierre begins to behave like the love-crazed hero of a classic romance.

When on the next visit he finds no trace of Marinette, he drives at furious speed off the motorway on to country lanes. Repeating the name of her village, Lusigny-sur-Ouche, he can get no sense from hostile or cretinous-seeming locals. Maneuvring the juggernaut in narrow spaces grows increasingly hazardous and farcical. Using a wayside crucifix for support to pull the lorry out of mud, they knock it askew. They compound their blasphemous affront to religion by next violating civil worship, when they hack pieces off a war memorial. Pierre remarks caustically that statues of mutilated men should be placed in public squares, as a sign of what war actually involves.[4] The pair are then caught up in a celebration and a ludicrous punch-up, finally calmed down by Gaston. The revellers are young conscripts whooping it up before reporting in. Gaston had earlier included his experience in the Resistance in the general *connerie* of existence.[5] Luckily the young men are in a good mood and content themselves with a punning question about a huge lorry in the middle of nowhere: "Vous déménagez?" (Are you moving house/off your rockers?) (p. 296).

After all these frustrated attempts to find Marinette's village, Gaston understandably doubts whether it exists at all, or whether she was having Pierre on. While ready to admit that Lusigny might not exist, Pierre refuses to believe that the girl has played a cruel trick on him. Gaston counters that this makes no sense; and Pierre agrees, mysteriously: an imaginary girl would live in a nonexistent village. Gaston has in fact seen Marinette, so we know she is not a figment of Pierre's fancy.

The next day, Pierre stops the lorry opposite the rest area, on the other side of the four lanes, after beefing about the other drivers on the motorway, which he has not done before. We call this "motorway madness," but Pierre is about to set off on a particularly crazy form of it himself. He starts sprinting through the fast-moving traffic, heading for his bucolic spot. He is struck three times by different vehicles, "kicked around like a football," as Gaston describes it (p. 298). Before he dies Pierre is able to murmur the credo expressed earlier: Stay on the motorway, don't ever leave it. On its way off the A6, the ambulance passes a sign reading

"Lusigny-sur-Ouche: 0,5 km." Exactly as Marinette had said. When they had gone in search of her village and her, they had been on the wrong of the motorway. A simple mistake, but with lethal consequences. As Pierre had opined earlier, without realizing what it implied for him, ideals remain ideals only so long as you do not try to lay your hands on them. If he had been content to cruise up and down the A6, seeing the countryside through his sparkling windscreen, and Marinette through the fence, he would not now be dead. Not that she can be blamed for his fateful obsession with her. This is not, like "Tristan Vox," a story hostile to women. Pierre's terminal dimness is prepared for by Gaston's joshing him on this score at the beginning: "La grosse connerie chez moi, tu continues à la chercher? ... Je l'ai pas encore trouvée mais je la subodore" (p. 268). Despite his professed love of progress, Pierre was not cut out for change. As in "La Fin de Robinson Crusoé," youth (semi–imagined in Pierre's case) cannot be recaptured nor even, perhaps, be experienced properly in the first place.

Tournier describes himself as "un vagabond immobile," a stationary traveller. Though he has done a great deal of globetrotting, he probably believes that the best travel is in the imagination (a useful definition of literature). Perhaps petit Poucet had the best idea: lie on your bed and dream. However innocently, Pierre's lorry had provided the wrong kind of portage. Of course, Tournier knows in his writer's bones that he would have virtually nothing to write about if perfection reigned, if plenitude (largely imagined in "L'Aire du Muguet") had not given way to atomization. Above all else, writers desperately need original sin (or error), or they would have no function. Baudelaire thought the same about laughter.[6]

14
The Virtues of Perversion: "Le Fétichiste"

THE final piece in the collection is a dramatic monologue, with a few stage directions. It has been performed in Paris (produced by Olivier Hussenot), Berlin (Raymond Fuzellier), and London (Christopher Craig). It is highly histrionic in tone and content. Tournier once witnessed a performance of it in prison, at Fleury-Mérogis.[1] The starved inmates erupted in exaltation when the protagonist produced the stream of female underwear from his pockets. This text later became notorious when its New York production (Frederik Neumann) was promoted by a fetishists' club there. The subtitle, "Un acte pour un homme seul," is a double meaning: a one-act play for solo actor, or fetishism as the practice of a solitary man (there is no hint of onanism).

At least six likely reactions to this text come to mind:
• Disgust, accompanied by the desire to flog, castrate, or execute sexual deviants.
• Pity: Is it not melancholy to live a life based solely on substitutes?
• Unhealthy interest, drooling over the details.
• Waving of barge-pole: "This leaves me cold. I've never known anybody like this."
• Healthy interest: the reader tries to avoid feeling superior or condescending to the fetishist, whose idiosyncratic logic she or he tries to understand.
• Refusal to read the text at all. This is lazy, cowardly and illogical, as it prejudges the unknown.

The fact that the fetishist emerges from the audience to mount the stage implies that he is one of us, even if he has been singled out. The brotherly reader/spectator is hypocriticized. This man in the spotlight tells us he has one hour's parole: just enough for a one-act monologue. His obsession with clothes is made plain from the start, when he remarks that he enjoys seeing people—here, his predominantly bourgeois audience—all togged up. Clothes, he proposes equably, define us as human beings. This opinion is particularly pointed coming from a man let out for a brief spell from a psychiatric hospital, where he is frequently stripped—of dignity as well as of clothes, for in that context, nudity and shame are closely related: medical examinations, hydrotherapy, electroshock treatment.

There follows a brief moment of 1960s-style "happening" or psychodrama. The protagonist fancies he sees a loved woman in the auditorium, and comes down from the stage to seek her out. Henceforth, he will stay on stage, in the limelight, alone. He tells us how the asylum director trapped him into a Catch-22 situation, whereby the patient was judged sane enough to sign divorce papers, but too insane to be released. If his wife Antoinette wanted rid of him, he retains fond memories of her. The flashback begins.

His fetishistic fate started with a glove dropped by the girl next door (Antoinette), a vision in virginal white. Later, during his military service, her white panties cascade to her ankles as his cavalry troop is passing. Martin (a name in France of proverbial commonplaceness) is so overcome at the sight that he faints. A soldier passes out, though not like at St. Cyr. This is both comic and charming, varying as it does the macho stereotype. Brought round by a cloth steeped in surgical spirits, he is overjoyed to find that the cloth is in fact the panties. This fetish acts as a lucky charm when, during the 1939–45 War, Martin's cavalry squadron is decimated by German tanks. Captured, Martin undergoes in the Stalag close proximity with a body of men and their guards. He advances the theory that if the jackboots which distinguished the Nazis were taken away, mere men would remain. Martin's odd theories, like his whole lifestyle, go against the grain. Kindly in intention, this hypothesis can hardly be taken seriously.

As a prisoner, he took no advantage of the rare opportunities for orthodox sex. Women, in his eyes, are "takeaway," not to be consumed on the spot. In fact, what he prizes above all is their smell, their aura. Given a chance of escaping from the camp, he blows it by swooning when in a van full of prisoners' dirty laundry. This time he faints from disgust, not delight. Not that he loathes men. The clothes were stone-cold. (Tournier himself seems totally unfazed by stinks, literal or metaphorical). It is human warmth

Martin values. He protests that the wrecking of the escape plan was not his fault. Nothing ever is. He is just made that way. In *Le Vent Paraclet*, Tournier proposes jokily that the contradiction between the left-wing stress on environment (broken home) and the right-wing stress on heredity (born evil) might be resolved by picturing the individual as 100 percent a product of the former and 100 percent of the latter. We know nothing of Martin's heredity or environment. He seems to have been born a fetishist, even if the realization did not dawn until his teens. Though such thinking—intrinsic propensity—is the perfect alibi for bad faith, Tournier is far less censorious than Sartre. His characters swivel between acting very willfully and giving way to some power they believe beyond their control. Martin's fate, he gladly confesses, is frills and furbelows (F, p. 312): that is, external to himself.

His first glimpse of Antoinette on return from captivity is of a figure in white organdy. His only regret is that she is not wearing a hat with a short veil, as he finds such semi-opaque accessories delectably troubling. Despite some doubts, he marries her. Should a man of destiny not remain single? Should he become a celibate priest? The skirts and underlayers of priestly garb do tempt him, but the total image is all too male, too reminiscent of beards and fathers—the only hint we have of Martin's childhood, possibly akin to Tupik's.

By a nice reversal of the cliché, the wedding night is a terrible trial for the groom rather than for the blushing bride. His first sight of her unclothed body brings to his mind and gorge meat on a butcher's slab. Averting his gaze, he buries his head with enormous relief in the pile of her clothes; he loses himself in the warm, sweet-smelling mass. Technically, he is not a fetishist, as he does not seem to use his fetish, clothes, in order to achieve sexual climax.[2] Only after telling his wife to get dressed and rushing out to get drunk is he able, later, to consummate the marriage. And that is the last we hear of conventional sexuality in this story.

Martin denies that he is a prude. A human body, for him, is only a peg, a model, to hang clothes on. (Dress designers and fashion photographers would sympathize with this view.) Antoinette becomes the best-dressed, or at least the most-dressed woman in town, as he supplies her with a constant stream of new clothes. This has its comic side, like his theories, distinguos and analogies, all of them disproportionate. Inviting us to smile occasionally at his oddball hero helps Tournier to make Martin less of a monster or pervert, in the normal senses of those words. Martin, for instance, buys a sexy brassière, but it is miles too big for Antoinette. Her petite breasts float around in it; reality is no match for imagination. After this minor fiasco, he memorizes her every measurement and updates them regularly. This effectively turns his wife into a sex-object, catalogued, taped. The escalation continues apace. He travels further afield, to Paris, in order to buy more exotic lingerie. Rather like dead souls in trees in the Celtic myth cherished by Proust, clothes on hooks in shops seem to call out to Martin to rescue them and take them home. Fetishism imprisons Martin, but it sets free clothes from mere functionality.

Well before now, readers must have started to wonder where the money comes from for such costly obsessions. An acolyte of "le démon de l'analogie," a lover of far-fetched conjunctions, Tournier blithely, or in unconscious self-parody, leapfrogs the gap between Martin's budgetary needs and his work in a bank: incinerating used banknotes, of which he hoards the ashes. The only connection offered is that of warmth (recently vacated underwear, recently handled, then burned, notes). Sexual excitement for Martin is essentially warm intimacy which, possibly—we are not told— he was denied as a child. Ashes, obviously, buy nothing. Martin moves on to collecting lost property. He calls the notes found inside wallets "billets couvés," hatched notes (p. 322). Wallets are often kept near the heart, or the buttocks. He jokes about the congealed sexual symbolism of wallets: testicles and scrotum. Is stealing wallets the next stage, a form of sodomy? No, only a means to the end of purchasing clothes. His fetishism moves into the areas of risk and illegality.

Thus, when he falls for the mauve satin bra of a cinema cashier, he imperils all, comically, to steal it from her flat. For the first time, he does not offer the prize to Antoinette. The bra is second-hand, and he dislikes promiscuity, mixing it. He imagines he possesses the ex-owner, without her or his wife knowing. It is secret power, and a new dimension. His next sortie is even more hazardous and public. He is "coming out," in effect. On the Paris métro, he mugs a woman for her black nylon suspender-belt which he has glimpsed. It is still tepid when he carries it off, as he says, like a scalp (p. 329). With him when all this happens, Antoinette understandably deserts him as a result. When Martin reads about his kinky hijack in the papers, it is clear that he is beginning to be labelled; he has become a *case*.

Admitting that any happiness he has known has been precarious, Martin claims he has had to construct his life, that it was not cut and dried for him as it is for most people. This argument directly contradicts his earlier plea that he is not responsible for his actions. Indeed, he wants to be caught and punished. Locked up for stealing lingerie, then released, he reoffends. He is then diagnosed officially as not responsible for his actions and locked up for good in an asylum. He has been there for twenty years and is no doubt by now thoroughly institutionalized. Life there, he emphasises, is no bed of roses, what with straitjackets, freezing showers, electroshock and drugs pumped into him. The consolations are the occasional day releases. Today he has been allowed to go to a clothes sale in a big store.

At this point, like a magician, the actor begins to pull out from his pockets a seemingly endless chain of female underwear, which he starts hanging out on a line. A flimsy Maginot Line with which to resist the incursions of the normal world. Still theorizing *in extremis,* he distinguishes between two types of lingerie: the clinging and the floating. Symbolist poets favoured *le flou.* Is Martin a poet, in his fanciful beating about the bush, his circumlocuting? For him, clinging underwear does not give the imagination enough free play. It is the loose that sets off dreams (p. 332). A veiled body is not a blunt statement; it is an allusion. In Martin coincide French classicism and decadentism. In Laclos's *Les Liaisons dangereuses,* Mme. Merteuil chooses a deliberate *négligé,* a *déshabillé* that "ne laisse rien voir et pourtant fait tout deviner."[3] Martin prefers the tantalizing to the glutting. Throughout, this lyrical *apologia pro vitio suo* is presented in nonpejorative terms of chatter *(bavardage).* This is what we listen to for one hour. This is what literature, viewed at its most basic level, is. For his part, Tournier freely admits to being a gasbag, in person or on paper.

The last part of the monologue rubs the audience's/reader's noses in Martin's obsession. We are converted into Peeping Toms; and, if readers, we have to imagine the scene, which ups our complicity. Authority closes in on the fetishist, as he rabbits on. The asylum attendants, the men in the white coats, have come for him. Witnesses of the scene are no doubt part horrified, part relieved. The officials advance slowly, menacingly. The lingerie floats in the breeze, thoughtfully provided by a wind machine in the wings. Martin comes to attention before the objects of his obsession, a kind of end-stopped erection that will lead nowhere. He scarcely possesses the spasmodic dignity of Abel Tiffauges, of whom Tournier could more confidently write: "Il n'y a sans doute rien de plus émouvant dans une vie d'homme que la découverte fortuite de la perversion à laquelle il est voué" (*RA*, p. 82). The genealogy of fetish is not brilliant: factitious. Compared with Tiffauges (vampirist, ogre, cannibal, coprophiliac, pedophiliac, necrophiliac, bestialist—even if largely on a platonic or metaphorical level), Martin is a monomaniac. In *Le Vent Paraclet*, Tournier, working to get Abel off the charge of perversion, claimed that the only true perverts are monomaniacs (*VP*, p. 122).

Though one of the joys of orthodox sex is rhythmic reiteration, Tournier does admit the monotony of perversion: "Le pervers est généralement bloqué dans un rituel qu'il ne peut que répéter après l'avoir mis au point."[4] Martin's version, however, does seem to attain the "répétition sans monotonie" sought by Abel Tiffauges (*RA*, p. 183). Asked whether authors practice what they preach, Tournier spoke in response of "surcompensation fabuleuse," and went on: "J'en connais un qui s'est aventuré presque partout et s'est toujours arrêté en chemin. Nécrophile impuissant, hétérosexuel sans lendemain, pédéraste raté, zoophile réticent, fétichiste indigent, coprophage pignocheur, pédophile sans patience" (*VP*, p. 123). This list, like many of Rabelais's, is essentially comic. Tournier *diverts* (and this very word has comic potentialities) perversion, so that it resembles more bifurcation, alternative routes.

As Martin's guard dogs reach the stage, he starts desperately gathering in his precious underwear. Checked, he persists, comes back for more, breaks away from the men. He *is* a fetishist. Nothing will ever stop him following through his passion. The last scene is black farce, and pathos, and very troubling. What harm is he doing to anyone? After all he is a nonsharer, hugging his goodies to himself, and not a proselytizer. Tournier shows here none of the loss of nerve that made him seek to convince us of "la portée humaine et universelle" of Abel Tiffauges's way-out obsessions (*VP*, p. 122). Martin is not a sadist; he has no designs on the flesh of women. Poignantly, he pleads to be spared electroshock on return to the asylum. He makes a last grab for some black briefs. The pirate's black flag? "Vive la mort!," he shouts,

14: THE VIRTUES OF PERVERSION

the age-old cry of the criminal outsider. Is his situation a living death, or a permanent revolt (cf. the other black flag—of anarchism)? Tournier may have had in mind Baudelaire's anguished, provocative note, attached to his jottings on Belgium:

> Je dis *Vive la Révolution* ! comme je dirais: *Vive la Destruction* ! *Vive l'Expiation* ! *Vive le Châtiment* ! *Vive la Mort* ! Non seulement je serais heureux d'être victime, mais je ne haïrais pas d'être bourreau—pour sentir la Révolution des deux manières ! Nous avons tous l'esprit républicain dans les veines, comme la vérole dans l'os, nous sommes démocratisés et syphilisés![5]

Martin, for his part, nails women's colors to his mast.

Who is mad here? As Maury has said, this fetishist lives according to the logic of his own mini-universe, to which supposedly normal people wish to have no access.[6] This playlet ends with all kinds of question marks. We could argue, perversely, that the fetishist is more pure, or puritanical, than most outside his asylum. After all, he prefers clothes to bodies, and clothes are the very emblem of civilization. His perversion is also a useful means of birth control. If the world produced a few more underwear-fetishists, it would have less overpopulation. Martin lifts on to a serio-comic level Tournier's fixation on sublimation. In the midst of his financial problems, he acquiesces in the daft suggestion of the old Jewish antiquarian, who maintains that, when Martin dies, his ashes will then come into full possession of the burned banknotes: "Des milliards en cendres, ça suppose un milliardaire en cendres" (p. 321). This is wordplay carried to absurd lengths. We could add: Martin is a kind of trusty, let out for the day. A pun is a trusty. It straddles two worlds of reference and begs to be accepted; but it remains suspect.

Tournier himself has claimed, perversely, that the norm is merely a generalized perversion unable to recognize the special norm of those deemed perverted. It is indeed often the case that society or its agents are more violent to deviants than many of these are to the community at large. Level-headedly, Weightman has declared that the fetishist here is "unfortunate. With a different application of his drives, he wouldn't have been locked up. He could have been a successful fashion photographer for luxury magazines."[7] Weightman argues further that there is not a great gap between a neurotic and a successful artist; the latter stands at one or two removes from his obsession. "And through the therapeutic business of symbolic transfer, maintains his balance and may, incidentally, earn his living through appealing to, and satisfying, the neurosis diffused throughout the normal public" (ibid.). The fact remains that, though Martin makes his private universe public, he hardly makes a work of art of it. And this, despite Tournier's repetition of Diderot's more justified claim in his studies of "monsters," that much profit can be gained for the understanding of ordinary experience by the sympathetic observation of the extraordinary (VP, p. 310–11).

Is this text pornographic, even softly so? Does this or that sentence, image, episode pull its weight as part of the total dramatic structure, or is it there simply for titillation? This text is certainly provocative, but that is its whole *raison d'être*. And it asks implicitly: Who shall throw the first stone? Tournier had an idea for a counterpart to "Le Fétichiste": *Le Voyeur*. An actor mimes to a tape (that is, his interior monologue), while peering through the keyhole of a movable door, sometimes back to audience, sometimes facing them. With a camera he takes flashes of the spectators which are instantly projected on slides on to a screen.[8] Such turning of the tables is largely latent in "Le Fétichiste" which, if it is pornographic, is so communally. A recently coined, euphonic, term in psychiatry for perversion is "paraphilia": deviant attraction. Its more loving hint would appeal to Tournier.

A pervert or monster can be defined only against a norm. He, or she, is reactive, against the grain. Tournier's self-imposed task is to present such deviation from the supposed norm as natural, existing in its own right. For him, monsters/perverts are creators of new or different moralities, alternative worlds. They can, like Lucien Gagneron, be dictators, but all suggest that the established world is not necessarily the only or best one. If this is special pleading, outsiders and minorities do have to defend themselves, or be defended by, special pleading. Just as garbage, in *Les Météores*, is meaningful and worthy of sustained attention, so the mental detritus of Martin needs to be heeded: Tournier as recuperator, if not redeemer.

He makes a special use of the word "logic":

Pour laisser libre cours à la folie raisonneuse et systématique, rien de tel que de donner directement la parole aux personnages. Alors le lecteur se trouve en tête à tête avec un homme qui s'explique, il est exposé de plein fouet à sa force de conviction, tandis que l'auteur caché, effacé, jouit en voyeur de ce face à face. (*VP*, p. 116)

Such strength of conviction can lead to that claim of infallibility that some Tournier protagonists do not fail to make, in an onset of papal bull. Not only in "Le Fétichiste" does the paucity of dialogue, the virtual absence of a gainsaying interlocutor, give rise to solo ranting. The fetishist is a Robinson without Vendredi. There is no Other to check and modify him.

If this fetishist seems not to desire the attainment of sexual release, he is clearly ready for imprisonment. He does not want to change. Paradoxically, he is an existentialist hero. Although he talks in terms of passivity (he cannot help it, he is made that way), in effect he chooses to persevere on his (twisting) path. He is more like Sartre's version of Jean Genet than Hoederer or Goetz. Nietzsche exploited the term *amor fati,* love of one's destiny, which suggests an active collaboration with the hand dealt us. The corollary of a totally meaning-full world, with its intricate network of signs, is, however, a diminution of individual freedom. A plethora of signs or symbols amounts to fate ("chock-full" comes from "choke"). When Tiffauges says of his "phoric" hands, made for bearing children, "tout cela prévu, voulu, agencé de toute éternité, et donc vénérable, adorable," it remains unclear who is the agency or willer (*RA*, p. 504). Yet Tournier's people are clearly propelled by imperious self-affirmation, come hell or high water, "contre vents et marées." It seems self-contradictory that Tournier professes to shun causalism, yet claims that his fictions provoke their own logical, even absurdly logical, conclusions, unless we accept that he substitutes his own arrogant causalism for the divine, materialist, or human variety. The result is curiously optimistic. When Alexandre in *Les Météores* talks of a force "qui va dans mon sens," he is celebrating a happy coincidence, commoner in Tournier's universe than tragic ones. This highly articulated universe, though leaving room in the mechanism for play, is "une machine infernale": "la machine subtile et irrésistible du destin" (*VP*, p. 241). Even those characters who plead they are fulfilling a pretraced destiny are provoking that finality; they are *agents provocateurs.* Tournier describes "amor fati" as "la force géniale d'un homme qui parvient à transformer en bénédiction un terrible coup du sort" (*VP*, pp.104–05). Against the orthodox view that lucidity accentuates tragedy, for Tournier "par la reconnaissance, le *fatum* devient amor fati" (*VP*, p. 242). His people bring it on themselves, like the protagonists of Flaubert's *Trois Contes*, in Tournier's view:

> Si le pessimisme est dépassé ici, c'est parce que chacun des héros des contes est l'auteur de sa propre histoire et le co-auteur de l'Histoire, ce qui n'exclut nullement au demeurant qu'elle le surprenne, le choque et le blesse, mais alors cette surprise, ce choc, cette blessure lui aura été infligée par lui-même. (*VV*, p. 173).

In his preface to the first publication of "Le Fétichiste," Tournier announced debonairly: "Le seul être dont je revendique absolument la place, c'est Dieu."[9] The novelist quâ God is the biggest leap of faith, the grandest approximation of them all. Is it too charitable to interpret this apparently monstrous ambition as a combination of a desire for absolute power, but coupled with the capacity for forgiveness? Not perhaps infinite forgiveness, but certainly the opposite of condemnation. Neither Heaven nor Hell, but Limbo—that ambiguous holding place to which people (especially unbaptized babes and ignorant, good-hearted heathens) are assigned without labels of final destination affixed to them. Tournier's characters are just such displaced persons. Above all, such godlike serenity would compare well with that of Luis Buñuel, who only at the age of sixty achieved the ideal of

> the perfect innocence of the imagination. It took that long for me to admit that whatever entered my head was my business and mine alone. The concept of sin or evil simply didn't apply; I was free to let my imagination go wherever it chose, even if it produced . . . hopelessly decadent ideas.[10]

15
The Play of Words

THIS title embraces, somewhat drunkenly, wordplay of several varieties (puns, oxymoron, irony, metaphor, symbol), just as "play" in mechanics means room for maneuver or approximate fit. Tournier's style, his rhetoric serve seriously and humorously his worldview. The provisional title of *Le Coq de bruyère, Mon Manteau d'images*, leaves it ambiguous whether Tournier drapes himself or his discourse in a blanket of words.[1] His prose is rarely woolly, but it frequently pulls the wool. His play has serious designs on us.

A highly figurative writer, Tournier suggests in all his work that we can do little else but offer metaphors: attempted unifications, mostly of an approximate kind. Metaphors make liaisons, often dangerous. As Paul says in *Les Météores*: "L'analogie s'impose, oui. Et elle va dans mon sens" (*M*, p. 44). Such *convenient* assumptions, expressed reflexively *(s'impose)*, as if to disclaim responsibility, to pass the buck, are characteristic of Tournier's personal ideology. Tournier loves placing apparently unmatched singles together in oxymoronic pairs (e.g., Lucien Gagneron and Bob, Pierre and Gaston), playing one off against the other, or playing between them, like a spark across a gap.

I have mentioned in individual sections functional or generative puns ("fermer les yeux," "avoir la peau"). There are other good reasons why Tournier is so drawn to punning, and a study of this wider question should help my general inquiry into the imaginable states of his mind. Just as his fetishist is a curious amalgam, an existentialist fatalist, committed to his destiny, so Tournier regards language, like Freud, as meeting us halfway, lending itself to our deeper purposes. Similarly, in photography, he notes the serendipity of the great exponents of the art, "le pouvoir inexplicable de susciter des coïncidences, des coups de chance, d'incroyables rencontres, où le hasard a d'autant moins sa part que ces miracles ne cessent de se produire en leur faveur, et en leur seule faveur." (*CM*, p. 64).[3] Tournier's often forced or far-fetched linkages (e.g., burnt banknotes/lingerie) are semantic puns. Life itself provides material for bizarre overlays and conjunctions, just as language houses acoustic coincidences. In both cases, the treasure trove lies waiting to be picked up and exploited by the gifted prospector.[4] Punners love language, are true philologers. Puns are the lovers *in* language, the separate words or phrases that realize secret affinities, exert reciprocal tugs and aid, as Dr. Johnson put it,"the unexpected copulation of ideas."[5] The androgyny patent in several of Tournier's stories is a further variation on overlap or alternation. "Coniunctio oppositorum," central to the Gnostic tradition and to Metaphysical poetry (which was under no doubts that puns can make full sense) nourishes many of Tournier's fictions.

Just as "suggestive" regrettably or not, has in English largely sexual connotations, so "équivoque" in French weds double meaning and flirting with moral danger. The overarching pun in *Le Roi des aulnes* is that on perversion: of youth, of language, of signs. Abel Tiffauges, leading a double life, plays dangerous games and is in effect himself an existential pun. Tournier works everywhere to abolish distances, distinctions, discriminations; he practices conflation. Just as he rejuvenates myth, and rehabilitates marginals (dwarfs, fetishists), so he recycles set expressions in a process of lexical revitalization which seeks to extract the maximum juice from words. "Il y a de grandes ressources pour le style ... dans la distorsion des locutions usuelles" (*VP*, p. 165). This alertness to automatisms (clichés, idioms) helps either as a springboard into fresh language, or as a danger signal about stale. It is, however, a warning sign to which Tournier himself often turns a blind eye. His liturgical word hoard ("inversion," "initiation," "affinité," etc.) is often marked by inertia, by unexamined values; such words are used then as magic talismans. Perhaps, like Carroll's Humpty Dumpty, that lexical taskmaster, Tournier should pay such "knock-down words" overtime.[6]

Tournier is naturally aware of the bad press puns habitually receive, and can write slightingly of them himself. Among the French deportees in *Le Roi des aulnes* is a Parisian *banlieusard*, Phiphi de Pantin, "qui fatiguait tout le monde de ses calembours et de ses grimaces" (*RA*, p. 259). As if to underscore the desperate nature of such mindless verbal mechanisms, Phiphi commits suicide shortly after "un feu d'artifices d'à-peu-près' (ibid., p. 272). Those were bad puns (like the vast majority in the workaday world), but *l'à-peu-près* is also a standard, nonpejorative word for a pun. Besides, even bad puns, Tournier recognizes, can be pointed: "Par un livre, un auteur se livre. Ce médiocre calembour va droit au coeur d'une vérité cruelle" (*VV*, p. 144). Tournier prefers pointed puns, justified puns, preferably backed up (however shakily) by etymology. He rarely apologizes (the cliché of punning is to say "Sorry!"). Finding polysemy is a cause of jubilation. An initially lugubrious portrait of the dying Sartre in *Petites Proses* is lit up by variant meanings, playing on *hêtre/être*: "Le livre et le hêtre ont des racines communes. ... En latin, *liber* veut dire écorce et livre. Ce n'est pas un hasard."[7] The fortuitousness of puns still has revelatory results. Language has some ideas of its own; it puts ideas in our heads.

More generally, Tournier seeks to justify puns by underlining their philosophical foundations. On the crystallographer Novalis and the crystallization of his love for Sophie, Tournier embroiders prettily:

> Il ne s'agit pas là d'un simple jeu de mots—stendhalien avant la lettre—ou plutôt nous sommes déjà avec Novalis dans ce courant qui dure encore (Heidegger) et pour lequel le calembour a valeur d'intuition métaphysique. Toutes les relations de Novalis et de sa fiancée tiennent dans cet aveu: "Je suis philosophe parce que j'aime Sophie." (*VV*, p.71)

Novalis' contemporary, Hölderlin, "savait, lui, laisser les mots jouer leur jeu divin" (*VV*, p. 73). Another, Jean-Paul, located part of the seduction of puns in

> the surprise at the element of chance which runs through the world playing with sound. As a wild coupling without priest, every coincidence pleases us, perhaps because the very idea of causality half-hiding and half-revealing itself seems like wit to wed the dissimilar.[8]

Illicit couples, the role of chance, the downplaying of causalism, the ambiance of black masses, all these elements link up with Tournier. God himself is possibly a prankster mountebank, "un démiurge baroque poussé aux plus folles combinaisons par l'ange du bizarre" (*VLP*, p. 120).

When Robinson declares: "Je ne puis plus parler qu'à la lettre" (*VLP*, p. 68), he steps out of line with his creator and his fictional brothers. Tournier retains enough of his Catholic indoctrination to believe that puns are, in both senses, divine, because of transubstantiation: the spiritual inhering in the physical, the figurative in the literal. Puns play in the space between abstract and concrete, the letter and the spirit, between which there is seldom any one-way traffic, but rather a shuttle.

Tournier's Robinson on his island longs for grace both theological and balletic and, after Nietzsche, prays: "Délivre-moi de la gravité" (*VLP*, p. 217). Puns enable hilarity (think of Mélanie) to be consubstantial with, part and parcel of, deadly seriousness; to have it both ways—the hallmark of the pun. Such games have their real risks. Playing with words is dangerous for the player, the receiver, and the stability or the self-satisfaction of unambiguous language. "*Chic* vient de *chicane,* et cela dit assez les contraintes et les contournements, les entraves et les contorsions qu'il impose."[9] A perfect example of such excruciation is: "J'ai compris qu'un genou blessé, "couronné" [grazed] devient par la magie des mots un genou royal."[10] If you are that way inclined, you do not need verbal magic to convince you. If you are not, such an accidental doublet will not persuade you. The pun is often such a *trompe-l'oeil*. Undeniably, wordplay can stem from a shortage of patience, a greedy cramming, and a refusal to look prosaic facts straight in the face. All in all, Tournier could second Abel Tiffauges's "double exigence de rigueur et d'aléa" (*RA*, p. 505). Systematization plus randomness: a useful definition of the paronym or approximate pun which, like text and photo, can set up "a distant counterpoint."[11]

Tournier often uses the word "affinités" as a bonding agent, and seeks to imply that such affinities are elective, beyond his control. For Galen Strawson, on the contrary, "Tournier is the master of the massively ramified conceit."[12] There is something devilish about his symbols. In *Le Roi des aulnes*, he coins an antonym to *symbole: diabole*, which he defines as "un signe qui désunit."[13] Tournier's fictional universe is, like Bachelard's material world, extremely communicative, chatterbox even. His signs and symbols partake of the generally ludic strain in his vision, so much so that the reader is tempted at times to mouth Gide's debonair pseudo-dialogue: "'Votre livre est trop plein de symboles—C'est pour me moquer des symboles'."[14] Saturation leads to deconstruction. Tournier inverts Blake's dictum, so that the road to wisdom leads to the palace of excess. Jankélévitch talks of "l'homéopathie de la surenchère," by which he stresses a self-regulating agency in the midst of surfeit, a check on escalation.[15] Comparably, Tournier's exaggeration (inflation/conflation) often reminds me of the fail-safe, pulled-punch variety of Jewish cursing ("May he go blind, God forbid!"), though he never lets prosaic inconveniences act as a brake on his freewheeling imagination. Tournier's texts are a semiologist's goldmine (and minefield). Semiology shades into the semaphore; the discreet bloats into the blatant. There is a bondage between certain kinds of wordplay such as that of Tournier, and high camp.

Structure

Tournier's symbols and leitmotifs yodel to each other across the intervening space of narrative. In structuring his stories, Tournier often exploits narrative blanks. The return journey in search of the island in "La Fin de Robinson Crusoé"; the temporal gap towards the end of "Les Suaires de Véronique" (what has she done with Hector?); the children-only performance, not described, in "Le Nain rouge"; the Fall, spirited away, in "La Famille Adam." Some of these gaps can no doubt be plausibly filled in by the reader. Some, no doubt, Tournier could not be bothered writing; it is the aftermath that interests him. Some are there as mysteries, something beyond words. Indeed, as the student Tournier wrote: "Il faut . . . ne pas croire qu'expliciter soit expliquer."[16] Language can go so far and no further.

The stories proceed often by lurches, depending on metaphorical swings and roundabouts (see "Le Fétichiste" in particular). Everywhere, Tournier tries to persuade us that his frequently heterogeneous propositions all cohere, for, like the arm-chancing founding fathers of the American Revolution, if they do not hang together, they will assuredly hang separately. Remarking once that certain novelists love pretending that their characters escape their control and have to be tailed by their creators, Tournier stresses his own difference: "C'est le mécanisme mythologique et symbolique qui est si contraignant qu'il détermine entièrement l'action des personnages."[17] As with etymologies, puns, coincidences,

Tournier here again appears to abdicate responsibility for the infernal machine set up in his fictions (see "La Jeune Fille et la mort" and "Tupik").[18] Yet the final solution which liquidates his personages is a result of his initial decision. He, after all, imagines, rehearses the genocidal dreams of Lucien or Mélanie.

The Reader's Part

I touched on the question of writer-reader relationships in the section on "Tristan Vox." Puns, above all, require a reader, or listener, to register them, to twig. Indeed, just as puns involve a double take, so all of Tournier's works, he claims, unlike Gide who wanted merely to be reread, "doivent être reconnus—relus—dès la première lecture" (VP, p. 189). A kind of speeded-up action-replay. He puns on his own production: "L'oeuvre, l'oeuvre pie, la pieuvre" (VP, p. 184). He makes preemptive strikes.

He adores having his cake and eating it. Though he has suggested frequently that half the meaning of a text, or rather the completion of a text, rests in the hands of the reader, he still tries to control what we receivers think. Even when he is modest, he is immodestly so. He clearly wants to needle the vestigial morality, test the surviving shockability, of a by now permissive readership. Most deeply, he wants to be "maître de la pluie et du beau temps," eager to supplant, or at least to ape, God. There is something essentially comic about the attempt of writers as different and as similar as Tournier, Barthes or Gide to escape the prison houses they build themselves but which they blame on their public. "La fuite en avant," rather than killing off the author, leaves the critical camp follower or the reader for dead in a pursuit race. For his part, Tournier jams the airwaves, via numerous interviews or other explanations of his works. He is his own best deconstructionist, that is, conservationist.

Worton lengthily argues that Tournier uses so many different and clashing metaphors for the author/text–reader relationship that his account ends up unparaphrasable and disconcerting.[19] I would add that Tournier's very deliberate aim is precisely to *confondre*, in both senses: to discomfit, to put the reader through it, and to confuse, to amalgamate (as in the themes of unisex and reversal of signs). The complexities of his views on the relationship are tightly connected with those on "amor fati": a willed fate, a mixture of freedom and dependence. The writer cannot manage without readers' collaboration, but aims to dominate them.

For many readers, Tournier is too much. His strategy is one of blanket-bombing. He loves piling it on thick. This provokes often excessive, polarized responses from readers. He goes on today writing like an arch angel, "un archange du bizarre." His sumptuous prose seduces, irritates, and on occasion turns stomachs. Gamey, well-hung (in a different sense from that applied to Lucien Gagneron), his profusion can stink in many nostrils.

Conclusions

ONE of the major themes of *Le Coq de bruyère* is initiation; it takes several forms. Tupik, under-initiated, mutilates his present body for fear of his future self. Amandine is excitedly expectant but troubled, after guidance from the non-human world. Robinson's is a reverse initiation, a saddening introduction to old age and imaginative impotence. The Baron in "Le Coq de bruyère" similarly, enjoys a last spring before a bleak and terminal winter. Lucien Gagneron, we are lead to believe, has found his way to his true, beneficial vocation as a laughter-maker instead of as a butt. Raphaël Bidoche hangs in suspension, possibly ascending, possibly about to resink. Cain has finished his learning process and teaches God a salutary lesson. Hector has died from the experiments in creativity; and it is hard to imagine where Véronique could next proceed. Mélanie lies dead; she has achieved the ultimate, longed-for initiation. Pierre lies dying, after mistaking his objectives. Félix Robinet's world has shrunk. Petit Poucet enjoys a permanent escape route, though technically captive. The Fetishist will go on resisting all attempts to straitjacket him into sexual normality. Mother Christmas has initiated a whole community into the joys of peaceful coexistence. Initiation, clearly, brings no automatic profit, but it is, for Tournier, an ineluctable fact of life. Contrasting *Le Rouge et le Noir* (where a felt lack dynamizes the hero) with *La Nouvelle Héloïse* ("d'un statisme absolument affreux"), Tournier claims: "Je crois que je n'écrirai jamais un roman stagnant."[1] Movement out and onwards into experience, at whatever cost, dictates his narratives. If initiation usually involves secrecy, Tournier's version centers on open secrets (the oxymoron again), or half-open ones (tipping the wink): paradoxes, coexisting possibilities, as in Amandine's bittersweet experience.

Many readers find Tournier's protagonists special cases—and the Fetishist, Véronique, Mélanie or Lucien pathologically so. Undoubtedly eccentric, they can still illuminate more average experience, just as scientists and sociologists sometimes use "negative controls," studying the normal via the abnormal. "Tristan Vox" and "Le Coq de bruyère" illustrate, besides, just two of the ways in which Tournier returns indefatigably to the unregenerate fictions that breed in *all* our heads. Tournier is rare in twentieth-century fiction (Giono is another) in being primarily a celebratory writer. Here is his own obituary:

> S'il lui fallait un ancêtre et une étiquette, on pourrait songer à J.-K. Huysmans et à celle de *naturaliste mystique*. C'est qu'à ses yeux tout est beau, même la laideur; tout est sacré, même la boue. (*CS*, p. 194)

While Mother Theresa could conceivably utter this with a straight face, Tournier is living here at least partly off unearned income. Indeed, for a wordplayer like him, there is no such thing as waste matter. Rubbish and brains, in French, can be covered by the same phrase, "matière grise" (see *M*, p. 99). He has, it is true, the grace to admit his gasbaggage (the French after all invented the hot-air balloon). No wonder Tournier is so taken with the Paraclete. A self-confessed rival to God, he bestows on his creatures a gift of generally divine speech. This also enables him, of course, to sound off through them, to ventriloquate. All the same, Tournier often invokes a different, troubling sound, the silent, wordless scream we can all hear at times in our heads or in the world about us.[2] This is most palpable in "La Jeune Fille et la mort," though that same story also enthrones laughter, a countervailing sound, as sublimity. Weightman relishes in *Le Coq de bruyère* "a dominant tone . . . of wild hilarity at the inextricable blend of ordinariness and strangeness in the world, a tone very unlike the gothic solemnity which now makes Poe, for instance, seem rather old-fashioned."[3]

Despite his undeniable hyperbolism, Tournier rejects blatancy. "Le noyautage, mes frères, le noyautage! . . . Baudelaire avec ses cheveux teints en vert a moins fait contre le système que le propret Kafka."[4] He makes a diabolic attempt to be on the side of the angels, pleading for love and for protection of the disadvantaged. Some sceptical readers feel that, for all his provocations, however, he never truly abandons safe ground; he plays at being diabolical, the devil's advocate. It is certainly true that he rarely seems to think against himself. His left hand generally knows, perhaps too well, what his right hand is up to. There is far more monologue than dialogue in all of his fiction, "Le Fétichiste" being only the most extreme example of this. Soliloquies suit tyrants. Whether he actively seconds his characters' extravagances or not, he certainly (see "Les Suaires de Véronique") acts the fellow-traveller. Nevertheless, he seldom seems cozily "politically correct" when he refuses to add his sputum to the spat-upon. He has a permanent dilemma: how to affirm without appearing to proselytize? How to promote the individual without harming the collectivity? His standard defense, of course, is that it is his over-the-top protagonists who generalize like the plague. Like Mélanie, he himself surely knows in his heart of hearts that he excels at finding instances (discrete phenomena) rather than unassailable proofs. "Une hypothèse ... qui trouverait sans doute d'innombrables illustrations à défaut de démonstration" (*VV*, p. 51). Again, proliferation and approximation, rather than pedantry.

Tournier wants to teach us lessons, even if the subtext of his messages is that we should withstand all attempts, even his, to brainwash us. A listing of what Fergusson wittily calls his "gene pool" is daunting: "Plato's ontology, Spinoza's epistemology and ethics, Sartre's *objecticité*, Kant's noumenon, Hegelian dialectic, Leibnizian harmony, St. Anselm's logic, Nietzschean joy and Heideggerian wonder."[5] How does Tournier breathe beneath such a load? Mélanie's unimpressed reaction to such love of philosophical re-expatiation is instructive and healthy, as is Idriss listening to erudite disquisitions on his native Sahara: "Les Français, faut toujours qu'ils expliquent tout. Mais moi, je comprends rien à leurs explications" (*GO*, p. 151). Such responses are not those of anti–intellectual Luddites, for the highly sophisticated Alexandre also asks this awkward question about his own alambicated lucubrations: "Tout cela est fort bien, mais ne s'agit-il pas d'une simple construction de l'esprit? (*M*, p. 382). Obviously, all literature is a mental construct; it does not just happen. Few readers, however, want to collide with the scaffolding. A suspicion lingers, all the same, that Tournier hankers after Prelati's "raisonnements spécieux mais inattaquables" (*GJ*, p. 75).[6] The bald Tournier has *un fier toupet*.

In Tournier, opposites are rarely polar. They are most often "oppos" (opposite numbers, mates), even twins. Mélanie is no misanthrope. Pierre and Gaston, very different in temperaments, are true friends. Even though Tournier exploits binary patterns, he arranges interchange, interplay, overlap between them. And contamination. A common error is to think of "serious" and "playful" as mutually exclusive, whereas each is a mode of the other. Gravity is earth-bound without levity. Poets practice *enjambement*.

I said at the outset that in small fictions Tournier still thinks big. Where short stories are so often consciously minor and tight-lipped, Tournier stretches the form and packs it tight. Perhaps like Ambrose Bierce, he could say: "Novel: A short story padded."[7]

Teeth set on edge and sickly grins must be common reactions to Tournier's fictions, alternating with silent whistles of admiration and wonderment for the feats he can pull off. He offers a mixed bag: sights for sore eyes, cloying of the palate, refreshment of jaded minds. His very eagerness to communicate makes him at times, like Véronique, an opinionator, a barrack's room lawyer, a bar bore. He can often appear, too, a metaphysical playboy, reminiscent of Musset's Fantasio ("Je suis en train de bouleverser l'univers pour le mettre en acrostiche").[8] However flirtatious his ploys, they are as often as not, like those of Alexandre, "à rebrousse-poil" (*M*, p. 40).

Here is a reasoned criticism of the collection as a whole:

> Rien n'est laissé au hasard dans cet univers où l'imagination romanesque expose, dans un style presque dogmatique, un arsenal de fantasmes bien huilés, une tératologie perfectionnée, un jardin secret aux allées soigneusement ratissées. C'est tout de même étrange, cette impression de fini, de *léché*. Jamais cet écrivain si obstinément français ne semble surpris par ce qu'il lui arrive d'écrire.[9]

The last sentence intrigues. How can we ever know? Alexandre claims to be surprised at times by himself even when he has long cultivated what will eventually amaze him. Despite many anti-modern reflexes, Tournier is a postmodernist with the best and worst of them. A joky consumerist verdict seems apposite: "Can you wonder that in France and elsewhere they are still trying to decide if Tournier is the greatest thing since sliced Sartre, or not?."[10] Playing with mathematical signs like Tournier himself, we could conclude that he is, more or less, a genius.

Notes

Preface

1. J.-J. Brochier, "Dix-huit Questions à Michel Tournier," *Magazine littéraire*, 138 (1978): 12.
2. "Rencontre avec Michel Tournier," *Rapports* 58 (1988): 148.
3. B. Bettelheim, *The Uses of Enchantment* (London, 1976), 168.
4. Quoted in Brochier, "Dix-huit Questions," 12.
5. T. Todorov, "Introduction à la symbolique," *Poétique* 11 (1972): 290.

Chapter 1. The Founding Myth

1. For multiple variants on the Adam/Eve topos, see J.-B. Vray, "La Question de l'origine," in *Images et signes de Michel Tournier*, edited by A. Bouloumié and M. de Gandillac (Paris, 1991), 58–62.
2. In 1992, British Methodists voted to make God, or at least the pronouns used to refer to the deity, of optional gender.
3. It is a comic writer, Aristophanes, on whom Plato fathers the myth in his *Symposium*. Aristophanes hiccups and sneezes before performing.
4. See Tournier's review of Jacob's *Le Jeu des possibles*, *Le Monde*, 8–9 November 1981, 7; and Jacob, "Evolution and Tinkering," *Science*, 196 (1977), 1164.
5. For a conspectus, see R. Le Senne, *Traité de caractérologie* (Paris, 1963).
6. V. Hugo, "La Conscience," *La Légende des siècles*.
7. H. D. Thoreau, *Walden* (New York, 1960) 211.
8. C. Baroche, "L'Eternel Retour à l'enfance," in *Images et signes de Michel Tournier*, 80.
9. C. Davis, *Michel Tournier: Philosophy and Fiction* (Oxford, 1988), 192.

Chapter 2. Closure of the Myth

1. "Aft-boding" coined by Ogden Nash, "If a Boder Meets a Boder, Need a Boder Cry? Yes," *There's Always Another Windmill* (Harmondsworth, 1972), 69.

Chapter 3. Creation of Legend

1. *Elle*, 16 December 1974, 14–16.
2. See S. Petit, *Michel Tournier's Metaphysical Fictions* (Amsterdam/Philadelphia, 1991), 103.

Chapter 4. The Good Initiation

1. This story is dedicated to the young daughter of a photographer friend, Lucien Clergue, who crops up in "Les Suaires de Véronique."

2. Rousseau, *Emile,* edited by F. and P. Richard (Paris, 1957), 176.
3. "Rencontre avec Michel Tournier," 153.
4. This interview, 9 December 1977, is reprinted at the back of the Folio edition of *Le Coq de bruyère,* 337–40.
5. A. Purdy points out that the name Amandine derives from *amande,* which is linked etymologically to *amygdale.* "The Essential Michel Tournier: Paradigm or Paradox?" *Dalhousie French Studies,* 12 (1987), 64. Her initiation is, however, obviously far less violently bloody than Tournier's.
6. M. Proust, *Contre Sainte-Beuve* (Paris, 1954), 368.

Chapter 5. Child Father to Man

1. See C. Perrault, *Contes* (Paris, 1989), 286–93. In *Gilles et Jeanne,* pp. 53–55, Tournier retells a more standard version of this tale. But the castle Poucet climbs a tree to see is Tiffauges, home of Gilles de Rais. A smell of black smoke and incinerated flesh hovers in the air. Gilles asks: "Est-ce une odeur de fagot ou une odeur de sainteté? *Gilles et Jeanne* thus involves even folktale children in its moral monstrosities and ambiguities.
2. This story was first published in *Elle,* 18 December 1972, pp. 120–26, as "Le Détournement du petit Poucet." "Détournement" suggests the father's attempt to denature him; the boy's act of bifurcation; and his "abduction" by kindly Logre and his winsome daughters.
3. An in-joke possibly operates here. In Sartre's *La Nausée,* a chestnut tree, a Tree of Ignorance, forces home to Roquentin the message of the senseless proliferation of matter. Tournier is on record as preferring trees even to animals. See A. Bouloumié, "Tournier face aux lycéens," *Magazine littéraire* (January 1986), 23.
4. J. Paulhan, "Le Bonheur dans l'esclavage," preface to P. Réage, *Histoire d'O* (Paris, 1954), iv.
5. Cf. A. Bierce, turning the tables: "God made the world in six days and was arrested on the seventh," *The Devil's Dictionary,* in *Collected Writings* (London, 1988), 352.
6. A. Bouloumié, *Michel Tournier: Le Roman mythologique* (Paris, 1988), 104.
7. See his *The Uses of Enchantment,* 116 ff.

Chapter 6. Sex and Confusion

1. The name Cromorne was that of Abel Tiffauges in the first draft of *Le Roi des aulnes.* Tournier liked the Germanic resonance of the word *cromorne* (krummhorn, a curved wind instrument). *Idola cromornia* was the title of a projected book of photographs purportedly taken by Cromorne, but never published. (Letter from Tournier, 4 August 1992).
2. B. Bettelheim, *Symbolic Wounds: Puberty Rites and the Envious Male* (London, 1955), 63.
3. Tournier, "Journal extime (suite)," *Sud,* 61 (1986), pp. 179–80.
4. Tournier, "Variations sadiques," *Le Monde,* 10 October 1986, 13.

Chapter 7. The Optative Mode

1. M. Worton, *Michel Tournier: "La Goutte d'or,"* (Glasgow, 1992), 34.

Chapter 8. Purifying Laughter

1. Dwarfism as a medical condition, caused by insufficient growth hormones, some kinds of heart or liver disease, or on occasion by emotional deprivation, seems not to interest Tournier here. In an interview, Tournier stressed that "Le Nain rouge" sprang from an idea, not from a *fait-divers* ("Ça sent l'empirique"). In the best/worst French tradition, Tournier, when on his high horse at least, toffee-noses empiricism. See Brochier, "Dix-huit Questions à Michel Tournier," 13.

2. S. Koster, *Michel Tournier* (Paris, 1986), 74.

3. Cf. Anne Sexton: "The dwarfs, those little hot dogs," "Snow White and the Seven dwarfs," *Transformations* (Boston, 1971), 6.

4. See A. Poirson, "Une Logique contre vents et marées," *La Nouvelle Critique,* 105 (1977), 48.

5. While Tournier would predictably prefer the white clown, cultivating insolence, persiflage, irony and double entendre, the red clown has his day when he contrasts Rousseau and Napoleon (red) with Voltaire and Talleyrand (white). The latter two are made to sound mean-spirited: "Les témoins sarcastiques de leur temps, les diplomates, les calculateurs, tous ceux qui veulent observer et manœuvrer sans s'exposer, gagner sans mettre en jeu leur liberté, leurs biens ni leur personne" (*CS*, pp. 73–75). Though like these two a self-professed *noyauteur,* Tournier is also an exhibitionist.

6. B. Bettelheim, *The Uses of Enchantment,* 200.

7. Cf. "On peut concevoir une espèce de pansexualisme qui serait l'idéal." Interview with H. Marsan and Y. Charfe, "Un Ogre bien tranquille," *Gai Pied,* 23 (1981), 13.

8. R. Queneau, *Les Fleurs bleues,* (Paris, 1978), 42: "Ne néologise pas toi-même: c'est là privilège de duc."

9. In the U.S., Sartre was nicknamed "Mr. Five-by-five."

10. In Koster, ibid., p. 150, this does not stop Tournier from piling it on thick: "Dans 'Le Nain rouge' la révolution qualitative qui survient à la suite d'un processus continu quantitatif,—brusquement l'homme petit devient un nain,—c'est du pur Hegel."

11. In the same novel, Tournier points out with unconcealed delight that in armorial bearings right is left, and vice versa. In a similar vein, commenting on Yeats's lines, "For nothing can be sole or whole / That has not been rent," R. P. Blackmur states: "It is an enantiodromia, the shocked condition, the turning point, where a thing *becomes* its opposite," *Form and Value in Modern Poetry* (Garden City, 1957), 76. Furthermore, Roberts reminds us that *bricolage* often entails using materials "upside-down, back to front or inside out, in order to fit them into the new structure for which they are intended." M. D. Roberts, "Tournier, *bricolage* and the Mythical Imagination" (Cambridge, 1989), 93. Tournier learnt from Lévi-Strauss about the mythical aspects of bricolage. See *La Pensée sauvage* (Paris, 1962), 26. Finally, in Andersen's *The Snow Queen,* the diabolical distorting mirror changes each thing into its opposite (see *VP,* 49–52).

12. Brochier, "Dix-huit Questions à Michel Tournier," 12.

Chapter 9. Radio Daze and Imperishable Myth

1. Almost certainly one of those in-significant names, with which Tournier at times teases readers he has already drilled to seek out "speaking names."

2. Though not, as in Clint Eastwood's film, *Play Misty for Me*, actually seeking to kill the object of their fixation, their radio romance.
3. K. K. Ruthven, *Myth* (London, 1976), 44.
4. J.-L. Ezine, "Michel Tournier," *Les Nouvelles littéraires*, 2–8 June 1975, 3.
5. See C. Lévi-Strauss, *La Pensée sauvage* (Paris, 1962), 27 on the links between myth and intellectual *bricolage*. He stresses oblique approach, dodging maneuvers, parasitism and yet resultant creativity in such mental operations.
6. Tournier wrote a preface to the French translation of Goebbels' diaries (Paris, 1977).
7. See *VV*, 12–13, and *VP*, 184, for this theme and variations.

Chapter 10. Photographic Fetishism

1. Tiffauges buries his heart at wounded knees.
2. See "Création et prédation," *Cahiers de la photographie*, 8 (1982), 84ff., where Tournier admits to being the kind of photographer capable of taking but not of giving. A camera was his chief toy as a child, he told an interviewer on France-Inter, March 1992.
3. Tournier is ever conscious of the prehistory of words, their semantic density, the package of meanings gathered over the centuries.
4. cf. Abel Tiffauges, who finds the portage of a dead child far more onerous than a living one, but far more entrancing (*RA*, 539).
5. The English equivalent is more prosaic: "He who sleeps forgets his hunger."
6. When Balzac agreed to a daguerreotype in 1842, he explained to Nadar his theory:

Chaque corps dans la nature se trouve composé de séries de spectres, en couches superposées à l'infini, foliacées en pellicules infinitésimales. Chaque photographie est donc *l'épluchage* d'une de ces couches,—la plus superficielle,—et son application à plat sur la plaque photographique. Pour le corps photographié, il y a donc, lors de chaque prise de vue, perte évidente d'un de ces spectres, c'est-à-dire d'une part de son essence constitutive, épreuve redoutable. (*CM*, p. 28)

Balzac sounds here like the mad colonel in *Dr. Strangelove*.
7. Ever impenitent about displays of erudition, Tournier praised Novalis for incorporating his engineering and crystallographic expertise into his aspirations to the absolute. Similarly, Thomas Mann "se rattache certainement à cette aspiration totalisante qui ne veut rien laisser échapper du savoir humain" (*VV*, 298).
8. In *La Goutte d'or*, Idriss is comparably soaked in chemicals to generate dummies then used for shop windows and a peep show (*GO*, p. 217).
9. Tournier, "Yves Klein," *Le Tabor et le Sinaï* (Paris, 1988), 86–87. See also Roberts, "Tournier, *bricolage* and the Mythical Imagination" (interview with Tournier); and *Yves Klein, 1928–1962: A Retrospective* (Houston, 1982). Klein, whose work had mystic, Rosicrucian, and dadaist elements, and who was a judo expert, shares several heroes with Tournier: St. Sebastian, Gilles de Rais, Gaston Bachelard. Klein (ibid., p. 235) expounds a gentle theory of mutual thieving of ideas. Klein was said by Harold Rosenberg (quoted ibid., p. 27) to be "able to make a good show out of nothing" (cf. my chapter on "La Jeune Fille et la mort").
10. M. Rosello, *L'In-différence chez Michel Tournier* (Paris, 1990), 140. Reading, for Tournier, functions as a dry run (cf. "le coup sec" in *Les Météores*) for his own production.

11. In *Les Météores*, Alexandre Surin links his fate to that of young Eustache, because in criminal slang *surin* and *eustache* are synonyms for "knife." Alexandre will die stabbed in the rough-trade quarter of Casablanca.

12. In a letter of 4 August 1992, Tournier assured me that all the photographic experiments described were feasible, and had been executed by a Belgian photographer whose name he could not recall. . . . Rauschenberg, around 1949, produced "a monoprint made by exposing to light blueprint paper on which a nude woman was lying." Reported in *Yves Klein, 1928–1962*, 125.

13. M. Braudeau, "L'Ogre Tournier," *L'Express*, 29 May 1978, 147.

14. Anything less than whole philosophical systems was to the young Tournier and his cronies "strip-cartoons" (*VP*, p. 159).

15. Vera + *icon* mingles Latin and Greek, and makes the derivation questionable, which suits Tournier.

16. Tournier, foreword to *Miroirs: autoportraits* (Paris, 1973), n.p. (photos by Edouard Boubat).

17. Roberts, ibid., 106.

18. Experts tentatively agree with this etymology. Tournier goes on to link up with Baudelaire: the dandy, insolence and provocation.

19. Tournier, quoted by J. Garcin, "Michel Tournier: 'Un Film un peu tiède en regard de la nouvelle'," *Nouvelles littéraires*, 3 July 1980, 43.

20. Tournier, "Variations sadiques," 13.

21. J. Weightman, "Polymorphic Peter Pan," *New York Review of Books*, 31 (1984), 26.

22. Strabo quotes these words of Aristotle in his *Geography*, vol. 1X (London, 1929), 71. cf. Montherlant's life motto: "Aedificabo et destruam," *Service inutile* (Paris, 1973), 39.

Chapter 11. Something about Nothing

1. G. Lichtenberg, *Aphorisms*, trans. R. J. Hollingdale (Harmondsworth, 1990), 45.

2. J. Swift, *A Tale of a Tub and other Satires*, edited by K. Williams (London, 1982), 45.

3. P. Larkin, "I remember, I remember," *Collected Poems* (London, 1988), 81–82.

4. W. H. Auden, "In Memory of W. B. Yeats," *W. H. Auden* (Harmondsworth, 1958), 67.

5. Tournier discusses this story, which he envies greatly, in *VP*, 50.

6. See his interview with G. Dumur, "Portrait d'un ogre," *Le Nouvel Observateur*, 30 November 1970, 46. See also *VLP*, 28, for Robinson's waiting for his shipmates' putrescent corpses to become clean cadavers before decently burying them.

7. Cf. *CS*, 186: "Etre jeune, c'est n'avoir perdu personne encore."

8. Cf. all the animated cartoons featuring ever more elaborate and frustrated attempts to kill someone.

9. Elizabeth Barrett Browning, "Aurora Leigh," *Aurora Leigh and other poems*, edited by C. Kaplan (London, 1978), 245.

10. The more "normal" aging Baron in "Le Coq de bruyère" wonders whether his last-fling sexual bliss will finish him off.

11. I had the short-lived idea that Mélanie's stockpiling of weapons of destruction referred to the world's arms race. This is an example of over-interpretation, which Tournier, who often exceeds elegant sufficiency, seems to encourage in

his readers. Little else would warrant this reading, apart from the earlier allusion to the Cuban missile crisis. . . . A further example is significant/in-significant names. Is there any need to link Etienne's surname, Jonchet, with "jonchets," the game of spillikins, just because he delivers logs? The narrative frequently mentions "tranches" (lemon, bread), "le tranchant" of machines, "couleurs tranchantes" and "lames" (the "lamelles" of fungi). There is a dubious etymological link between the hybrid beast lamia and a gaping mouth, as in laughter. I have no wish to make an issue of any of this.

12. J. Starobinski, "Montaigne en mouvement (2)," *Nouvelle Revue Française*. 1 February 1960, 266. See *CS*, 171–75 re "la belle mort" and Tournier's wish to keep doctors and medicine at bargepole length.

13. P. Péju, *La Jeune Fille dans la forêt des contes* (Paris, 1981), 118.

14. The footnote to *JFM*, 196, pointing out that Coquebin's quotation about children as "ces demi-fous que nous tolérons parmi nous" comes from Pauline Réage's *Histoire d'O*, a pornographic classic, hints that his spirit of enquiry is not altogether pure.

15. L. Wittgenstein, *Tractatus Logico-Philosophicus*, translated by D. F. Pears and B.F. McGuinness (London, 1969), 3.

16. Wittgenstein, quoted in N. Malcolm, *Ludwig Wittgenstein* (Oxford, 1958), 29.

17. Tournier, "Les Mots sous les mots," *Le Débat*, 33 (1985), 97–98.

18. A. Koestler, *The Act of Creation* (London, 1964), 47.

19. Tournier, "Erudition et dérision," *Le Monde*, 6 June 1975, 18.

20. Reversing the telescope, Tournier writes of a neighbor's crying baby: "Cette petite plainte grêle me touche et me rassure. C'est la protestation du néant auquel on vient d'infliger l'existence" (*VI*, 7).

21. Cf. Beckett (after Democritus): "Nothing is more real than nothing," *Malone Dies* (London, 1968), 16, and the addendum to *Watt*: "Nothingness in words enclose" (London, 1963), 247.

22. R. Queneau, *Loin de Rueil* (Paris, 1976), 142, 145.

23. S. Fertig's coinage, in *Une Ecriture encyclopoétique: Formation et transformation chez Raymond Queneau* (University Microfilms, 1983), 27, re the musings of Saturnin in *Le Chiendent* on "le nonnête."

24. A. Bierce, *The Enlarged Devil's Dictionary* (Harmondsworth, 1967), 152

25. F. Brégis, "Michel Tournier n'est pas un romancier," *Brèves*, 10 (1983), 71.

26. F. Nietzsche, *Thus Spake Zarathustra*, trans. by R. J. Hollingdale (Harmondsworth, 1971), 201.

27. Tournier "Les Voyages initiatiques," *La Nouvelle Critique*, 105 (1977), 106.

28. Ibid. Novalis' *Heinrich von Ofterdingen* is Tournier's choice of the purest model of initiation novel.

29. A. Huxley, *Brave New World* (London, 1965), 64.

30. C. Davis, *Michel Tournier*, 8.

Chapter 12. The Fetish of Not Seeing

1. A grouse, or in Scotland capercaillie ("horse of the woods"). Grouse go in for elaborate courtship displays.

2. Compare the variant dreams of tyranny of Mélanie, Lucien Gagneron and the Fetishist. The baron's is more cameo-sized.

3. This is an alternative form of that initiation which is one of Tournier's recurrent themes. Initiation of others, in his scheme of things, is generally more coarsely self-centered than that of the self.

4. Freud's (1910) paper on "The Psycho-Analytic View of Psychogenic Disturbance of Vision" argues that "hysterical blindness can often be caused by sexual repression." See Freud, standard edition of *Complete Psychological Works,* edited by J. Strachey et al. (London, 1957), vol. 11, 211–18.

5. Contrast, for example, "La Jeune fille et la mort." After the publication of *La Goutte d'or,* Tournier appeared readier to countenance the possibly therapeutic effects of psychoanalysis, especially the "talking cure." "Songeons à la psychanalyse, cette espèce d'exorcisme de l'image par le verbe. C'est en parlant votre angoisse qu'elle se dissipe: un type de guérison par l'esprit." *L'Unité,* 4 February 1986.

6. Quoted in Brochier, "Dix-huit Questions à Michel Tournier," 12.

Chapter 13. Cain and Abel Revisited

1. Their home, Boullay-les-Troux, could translate as "Sod all dumps."
2. In the last stages of the Second World War, Tournier did his military service in Army transport, where he learned to maintain and drive twenty-ton lorries (*VP,* 85).
3. The lily-of-the-valley is traditionally associated with romance. An old verb *mugueter* meant to flirt or philander.
4. Cf. a similar idea, but applied to medals (of amputated legs, etc.) in Louis Guilloux's *Le Sang noir* (1935).
5. Cf. *VP,* p.80, for Tournier's own highly dismissive view of the Resistance.
6. See Baudelaire, "De l'Essence du rire," *Curiosités esthétiques.*

Chapter 14. The Virtues of Perversion

1. See Tournier, "Journal extime (suite)," 185–87.
2. Cf. Tournier's consistent belittling of genital sex. The penetrative aspects of sex, whether hetero- or homosexual, are of no interest to Martin.
3. Laclos, *Les Liaisons dangereuses,* edited by R. Pomeau (Paris, 1964), 37.
4. Tournier, "Je suis un métèque de la littérature," *Le Monde,* 28 March 1975, 16.
5. Baudelaire, *Oeuvres,* edited by Y. Le Dantec (Paris, 1951), vol. 2, 716. An ear as acute as Baudelaire's will have meant the pun *syphilisés/civilisés.*
6. P. Maury, "Michel Tournier ou la perversion du mythe," *Revue générale,* January 1977, 29.
7. J. Weightman, "Polymorphic Peter Pan," 25.
8. Tournier, *Journal de voyage au Canada* (Paris, 1984), 121–22. The photographer Boubat commented that this project was inspired by Tournier's spying on neighboring high-rise buildings from his hotel window (ibid., p.123).
9. In *La Quinzaine littéraire,* 190 (1974), 30.
10. L. Buñuel, *My Last Breath,* translated by A. Israel (London, 1985), 175.

Chapter 15. The Play of Words

1. Tournier, interviewed in *Elle,* 13 February 1978. The phrase is taken from a poem by Lanza del Vasto, which is also exploited, indeed embezzled, for the blurb.
2. See *Freud-Jung Letters,* translated by R. Manheim, edited by W. McGuire (London, 1974), 220, re this "linguistic compliance."
3. He is desciribing Lartigue. "Rencontre" is also an older term for "pun."

4. Tournier rejoices in "l'admirable ambiguïté du mot *inventer* qui veut dire couramment créer de toutes pièces, et, juridiquement, découvrir ce qui existait auparavant à l'état dissimulé (le code civil parle de 'l'inventeur d'un trésor')" (*VV*, p. 57).

5. Dr Johnson, *Rambler,* 194 (1752). cf. André Breton: "Les mots font l'amour," *Les Pas perdus* (Paris, 1924), 171.

6. Davis, *Michel Tournier,* p. 182, calls Tournier a word fetishist.

7. Tournier, *Petites Proses* (Paris, 1986), 165.

8. Jean Paul, *The Horn of Oberon,* translated by M. Hale (Detroit, 1973), 173, 178. The twins Jean and Paul in *Les Météores* are possibly a homage to this pathfinder.

9. Tournier, *Le Tabor et le Sinaï* (Paris, 1988), 177.

10. Tournier, "Variations sadiques," 13.

11. Blurb to *CS:* "Parfois la photographie flâne en marge de la réflexion qu'elle élargit et enrichit par un lointain contrepoint."

12. G. Strawson, "Piercing the many-coloured cloak," *Times Literary Supplement,* 16 October 1981, 1192.

13. Tournier, "Les Mots sous les mots," *Le Débat,* 33 (1985), 101. (In this text, a printer's devil, no doubt, put *diable*). In classical rhetoric, "diabole" is false accusation, slander, "to throw across" (cf. the roots of "metaphor": "to bear across"); "a prediction of (and sometimes a denunciation of) things that are to take place in the future." See R. A. Lanham, *A Handlist of Rhetorical Terms* (Berkeley/Los Angeles, 1960), 33. *Diable*/devil share the same derivation.

14. A. Gide, postface to *Paludes,* in *Romans* (Paris, 1958), 1477.

15. V. Jankélévitch, *L'Ironie* (Paris, 1950), 95.

16. Tournier's diploma thesis, "L'Intuition intellectuelle dans la philosophie de Platon" (p.12), quoted in K. Fergusson, *"La Recherche de l'absolu" in the works of Michel Tournier* (University of London, 1991), 81.

17. Tournier, interviewed by J.-L. Rambures, *Comment travaillent les écrivains* (Paris, 1978), 166. (Gide, Queneau, Unamuno would be examples of the other kind.)

18. Ibid., p. 167. Tournier has the grace to admit that a good novelist needs, like a Napoleonic general, good luck. Not only language but life itself needs to meet us halfway, by providing meaningful fortuities. He once noted that the date of the Hiroshima bomb, 6 August, was also that of the Transfiguration; the first was "une inversion maligne" of the second. (Quoted in A. Bouloumié, "Inversion bénigne, inversion maligne," in *Images et signes de Michel Tournier,* 35–36.

19. M.Worton, "Use and Abuse of Metaphor in Tournier's *Le Vol du vampire,*" *Paragraph* 10 (1987), pp. 13–28.

Conclusions

1. Quoted in B. Le Péchon, "Entretien avec M. Tournier," *Recherches sur l'imaginaire,* 5 (1979), 11.

2. See Davis, *Michel Tournier,* pp. 187–88. (cf. "le brame" in *RA*).

3. Weightman, "Polymorphic Peter Pan," 26.

4. Tournier, *Miroirs,* 192.

5. Fergusson, *"La Recherche de l'absolu" in the works of Michel Tournier,* 139.

6. Many critics respond in kind. Susan Petit devises an elaborate *grille* for *Le Coq de bruyère,* in which the first seven stories illustrate the cardinal virtues (three theological and four moral), and the last seven the deadly sins. With much

heaving and straining, it all fits. But so does *un cache-misère. Michel Tournier's Metaphysical Fictions* (Amsterdam/Philadelphia, 1991). A good example of overkill.

7. A. Bierce, 'The Devil's Dictionary,' *Collected Writings* (London, 1988), 313.

8. A. de Musset, *Fantasio*, in *Théâtre complet*, edited by M. Allem (Paris, 1958), 300.

9. C. David, "*Le Coq de bruyère*," *Le Nouvel Observateur*, 29 May 1978, 74.

10. H. Hebert, "Philosophy in Frills," *Guardian*, 12 November 1983, 8.

Bibliography

I have restricted the bibiography to those items most directly relevant to *Le Coq de bruyère* (Paris: Gallimard [Folio], 1981).

Arrouye, J. "Paraboles photographiques," *Sud,* 61 (1986): 154–60.
Baroche, C. "Vieux mythes et habit neuf," *Quinzaine littéraire* (16–31 May 1978): 7.
Bevan, D. "Tournier's Photographer: A Modern Bluebeard?" *Modern Language Studies* 15 (1985): 66–71.
———. *Michel Tournier* (Amsterdam: Rodopi, 1986).
Bouloumié, A. *Michel Tournier: Le Roman mythologique* (Paris: Corti, 1988).
Bouloumié, A. and M. de Gandillac, eds., *Images et signes de Michel Tournier* (Paris: Gallimard, 1991).
Braudeau, M. "L'Ogre Tournier," *L'Express,* 29 May 1978, 139, 163.
Brochier, J.-J. "Dix-huit Questions à Michel Tournier," *Magazine littéraire,* 138 (1978), 11–13.
Cartigny, M.-T. *"Le Coq de bruyère,"* *Francia,* 29 (1979), 71–73.
Cloonan, W. *Michel Tournier* (Boston: Twayne, 1985).
David, C. *"Le Coq de bruyère,"* *Le Nouvel Observateur,* 29 May 1978, 74.
Davis, C. *Michel Tournier: Philosophy and Fiction* (Oxford: Clarendon, 1988).
Debidour, V.-H. "Michel Tournier: *Le Coq de bruyère,*" *Bulletin des lettres,* 400 (1978), 252–53.
Easterlin, N. L. "Initiation and Counter-initiation: Progress towards adulthood in the stories of Michel Tournier," *Studies in Shorter Fiction,* 28 (1991), 151–68.
Enderlé, M. "L'Espace dans 'Le Nain rouge'", *Littératures,* 5 (1982), 111–16.
Fergusson, K. "Le Rire et l'absolu dans l'oeuvre de Michel Tournier," *Sud,* 61 (1986), 76–89.
———. "'La Recherche de l'absolu" in the works of Michel Tournier" (unpublished Ph.D. dissertation, University of London, 1991).
Fumaroli, M. "Michel Tournier et l'esprit d'enfance," *Commentaire,* 12 (1980–81), 638–43.
Garcin, J. "Un Film un peu tiède en regard de la nouvelle," *Nouvelles littéraires,* 3 July 1980, 43.
Guichard, N. *Michel Tournier: Autrui et la quête du double* (Paris: Didier, 1989).
Hayman, R. "Underwear and Tear," *TLS,* 25 November 1983, 1132.
Hebert, H. "Philosophy in Frills," *Guardian,* 12 November 1983, 8.
Jay, S. "Les Plumes du *Coq de bruyère,*" *Sud* (1980), 144–48.
Koster, S. *Michel Tournier* (Paris: Veyrier, 1986).

Le Péchon, B. "Entretien avec Michel Tournier," *Recherches sur l'imaginaire*, 5 (1979), 6–29.

Maclean, M. "Relationships in the Work of Michel Tournier" (unpublished Ph.D. dissertation, University of St. Andrews, 1985).

McMahon, J. "Michel Tournier's Texts for Children," *Children's Literature*, 13 (1985), 154–68.

Matignon, R. "Avec sa première pièce *Le Fétichiste:* Michel Tournier au masculin singulier," *Le Figaro,* 23 January 1975, 25.

Maury, P. "Michel Tournier: 'Le Nain rouge'," *Marginales,* September/October 1976, 57–59.

Merllié, F. *Michel Tournier* (Paris: Belfond, 1988).

Morillon, D. "De 'La Famille Adam' *(Le Coq de bruyère)* à l'oeuvre de Tournier," *Recheches sur l'imaginaire,* 10 (1983), 99–108.

Nourissier, F. "Le Fétichiste de Michel Tournier: pas assez fou," *Le Figaro,* 25 January 1975, 21.

Penrod, L. K. "Une Littérature initiatique: le refus du stéréotype dans 'Amandine ou les deux jardins de Michel Tournier'" in *Littérature pour la jeunesse: la croisée des chemins,* edited by D. Thaler (University of Victoria, B.C., 1988), 45–62.

Petit, S. *Michel Tournier's Metaphysical Fictions* (Amsterdam/Philadelphia: John Benjamin, 1991).

Piatier, J. "Michel Tournier sur la courte distance," *Le Monde,* 26 May 1978, 17.

Plumyène, J. "Un objet captivant," *Magazine littéraire,* 138 (1978), 22–23.

Redfern, W. D. "Approximating Man: Michel Tournier and Play in Language," *MLR,* 80 (1985), 304–19.

Roberts, M. D. "Tournier, *bricolage* and the Mythical Imagination" (unpublished Ph.D. dissertation, University of Cambridge, 1989).

Rosello, M. *L'In-différence chez Michel Tournier* (Paris: Corti, 1990).

Shattuck, R. *The Innocent Eye* (New York: Farrar, 1984), 205–18.

Spiteri, G. *"Le Coq de bruyère," Nouvelles littéraires,* 24 May 1978, 23–24.

Tournier, F. Kaye, M.-L. Girou-Swiderski, E. Roberto, N. Bourbonnais, D. Lafon and P.-L. Vaillancourt. *Incidences,* 2–3 (1979) "Analyse plurielle: 'Les Sueurs de Véronique.'"

Warehime, M. "Writing the Limits of Representation: Balzac, Zola and Tournier on Art and Photography," *SubStance,* 18 (1989), 51–57.

Weightman, J. "Polymorphic Peter Pan," *New York Review of Books,* 31 (1984), 25–26.

Wolfromm, D. "Tournier le détourneur," *Magazine littéraire,* 138 (1978), 24–25.

Worton, M. "Use and Abuse of Metaphor in Tournier's *Le Vol du vampire*," *Paragraph,* 10 (1987), 13–28.

Wright, B. "Charming but unpleasant," *TLS,* 13 October 1978, 1182.

Zeldin, T. "The Prophet of Unisex," *Observer,* 30 January 1983, 43.

Index

Abel (biblical), 12, 81, 96, 97
absolu,l', 82
Adam (biblical), 12, 17, 34, 122n.1
adults, 23, 26, 30, 35, 37, 38, 39, 40, 41, 78, 87. *See also* parents
Allais, Alphonse, 84
amor fati. See fate
amputation (mutilation), 38, 39, 40, 41, 49, 61, 64, 78, 88, 95, 99, 118
Andersen, Hans Christian, 11, 75, 124n.11, 126n.5
androgyne (hermaphrodite, bisexual, unisex), 17, 18, 21, 25, 27, 28, 29, 35, 40, 47, 52, 112, 116
animals, 26, 27, 28, 29, 31, 33
approximation, 17, 33, 104, 110, 111, 112, 115, 120
archetype, 46
Aristophanes, 122n.3
Arles, 62, 68, 69
art (writing), 43, 45, 52–53, 59, 60, 63, 64, 75, 85, 105, 108, 120
artist, 53, 54, 61, 66, 71, 74, 107–8
Aubry, Cécile, 90, 91
Auden, W. H., 74
author, 17, 50, 57, 58, 59, 61, 67, 78, 100, 106, 109, 110, 113, 115, 116, 121, 129n.18

Bach, Johann Sebastian, 14, 43
Bachelard, Gastor, 83, 114, 125n.9
Balzac, Honoré de, 125n.6
Baroche, Christiane, 20
Barthes, Roland, 116
Baudelaire, Charles, 100, 101, 107, 119, 126n.18, 128n.5
beard, 25, 37, 103
Beckett, Samuel, 125n.21
Bergson, Henri, 83
Bettelheim, Bruno, 36, 40, 51
Bibesco, Antoine, 76
Bible, 17, 18, 19, 25

Bierce, Ambrose, 86, 121, 123n.5
binary patterns, 13, 14, 26, 121
Blake, William, 115
blindness. *See* eyes
Bloom, Harold, 67
boredom *(ennui)*, 74, 75, 78, 81, 82, 88, 89, 90
Boubat, Edouard, 128n.8
Bouloumié, Arlette, 35
boy. *See* man
Breton, André, 129n.5
bricolage (recycling), 12, 18, 60, 67, 68, 75, 108, 112, 124n.11, 125n.2
Browning, Elizabeth Barrett, 80
bullfight, 69–70
Buñel, Luis, 110
Burns, Robert, 86

Cain (biblical), 12, 81, 96, 97
Camargue, 62–63, 69
Camus, Albert, 76, 88
caractérologie, 19
Carroll, Lewis, 84, 112
castration, 32, 35
causalism, 19, 53–54, 109, 113
Celini, Benvenuto, 65
chiasmus (criss-cross), 24, 30, 37
chic, 70, 114
child, 12, 14, 24, 26, 27, 29, 30, 31, 32, 34, 35, 36, 37, 38, 39, 40, 41, 42, 43, 47, 50, 51, 52, 65, 67, 75, 77, 79, 82, 90, 95, 104, 110, 127n.14
Christmas, 24, 32, 33, 34, 35, 42, 44, 51, 98
circus, 44, 49, 50, 51
Claudius, Matthias, 77
cliché (stereotype), 35, 43, 47, 49, 50, 52, 59, 60, 61, 63, 70, 74, 81, 83, 87, 92, 94, 98, 103, 112, 113
clothes, 101–2, 103, 104, 105, 105–6, 106, 107

133

Clergue, Lucien, 64, 122n.1
clown, 44, 46, 49, 50, 51, 73, 124n.5
coincidence, 49, 109, 111, 112, 113, 114, 115, 129n.18
Colette, (Sidonie-Gabrielle), 28
comedy. *See* humor
connerie, 96–97, 99, 100
conte, 11, 12, 14, 88, 94, 121
corpse (skeleton), 64, 65, 66, 76, 81, 83, 126n.6
Crusoe, Robinson, 12, 22

David, Catherine, 121
da Vinci, Leonardo, 65
Davis, Colin, 21, 88, 129n.6, 129n.2
death, 64, 65, 73, 74, 76, 76–77, 77, 78, 79, 80, 81, 82, 84, 85, 86, 87, 88, 106–7, 127n.12
deconstructionism, 115, 116
defamiliarization, 75
Defoe, Daniel, 22
'Deutsch', Nicholas Manuel, 77
devil, 24, 39, 43, 44, 45, 58, 85, 87, 113, 114, 119, 129n.13
dialogue, 109, 120
dictator, 47, 51, 60, 66, 70, 108, 120, 127n.2
didacticism (edification), 13, 52, 53, 66, 70, 80, 81, 83, 92, 94, 120, 121
Diderot, Denis, 108
Donne, John, 77
dwarf, 11, 36, 44, 46, 47, 48, 49, 50, 51, 52, 53, 54, 112, 124n.1

ecology, 34
Eden (Paradise), 20, 22, 23, 28, 34, 43. *See also* garden
edification. *See* didacticism
education (school), 19, 28, 30, 34, 37, 50, 73–74
eroticism. *See* sexuality
etymology, 13, 41, 63, 69, 70, 109, 113, 114, 115, 123n.5, 125n.3, 126n.15, 127n.11
euphemism (litotes), 46, 66, 91, 105
Eve (biblical), 12, 17, 18, 34, 122n.1
exaggeration, 40, 47, 52, 71, 85, 115, 117, 120, 126n.11
existentialism, 53, 88, 105, 109, 111, 119

eyes (blindness), 23, 44, 70, 80, 90, 92–93, 94, 95, 128n.4

fairy-stories, 35, 36, 57
Fall (Original Sin), 17, 18, 19, 100, 103, 115
fame, 42, 48, 49, 61
Father Christmas, 24, 25
fate *(amor fati)*, 31, 47, 48, 57, 58, 59, 87, 93, 96, 97, 100, 109, 109–10, 111, 115, 116–17
feminism, 31, 69, 81
Fergusson, Kirsty, 120
Fertig, Stanley, 127n.23
fetishism. *See* perversion
Flaubert, Gustave, 71, 110
flou, le, 105
freak. *See* monster
Freud, Sigmund, 40, 78, 93, 111, 128n.4, 128n.2

garden, 22, 27, 28, 29, 37, 38, 39, 41, 121
gender, 14, 17, 18, 19, 21, 25, 26, 27, 28, 29, 33, 37, 38, 39, 40, 50, 63
genocide, 48, 77, 78, 116
Gide, André, 13, 19, 114–15, 116, 129n.17
Giono, Jean, 28, 119
Gnosticism, 17, 112
God (god), 17, 18, 21, 34, 35, 43, 53, 55, 56, 63, 66, 71, 79, 82, 84, 85, 87, 109, 110, 113, 114, 116, 119, 122n.2, 123n.5
Goethe, Johann Wolfgang von, 77
Grass, Günter, 46
guardian-angel, 45, 91
guillotine, 78, 83, 85–86
Guilloux, Louis, 128n.4

habitat, 19
Hebert, Hugh, 121
Hegel, Georg Wilhelm Friedrich, 120
Heidegger, Martin, 88, 113, 120
Heraclitus, 81
heraldry, 42, 124n.11
hermaphrodite. *See* androgyne
hippy, 33, 35
Hiroshima, 67, 129n.18
Hirst, Damien, 73
Holy Ghost, 13, 18, 34, 119

INDEX

homosexuality. *See* sexuality
Hugo, Victor, 20
humor (comedy, wit), 13, 14, 17, 21, 24, 27, 50, 60, 74, 79, 82, 83, 84, 86, 87, 90, 91, 94, 97, 99, 100, 102, 103–4, 104, 106, 113, 116, 121
Huxley, Aldous, 88
Huysmans, Joris-Karl, 119
hybrid, 18, 38, 52

image, 55, 62, 66, 67, 68, 69, 70, 71, 72, 108
imitation. *See* plagiarism
initiation, 11, 14, 26, 27, 28, 29, 30, 31, 37, 38, 41, 58, 78, 80, 87–88, 112, 118, 123 n.4, 127 n.3
intertextuality, 12, 77
inversion, 25, 32, 47, 53, 61, 95, 112, 129 n.18
irony, 59, 72, 94, 111
island, 22, 23, 28, 115

Jacob, François, 19
Jankélévitch, Vladimir, 115
Jean-Paul (Richter), 113
Jesus Christ, 24, 35, 69
Johnson, Samuel, 112

Kafka, Franz, 119
Kant, Immanuel, 81, 120
Keillor, Garrison, 55
Klein, Yves, 67, 125 n.9
Koestler, Arthur, 83
Laclos, Choderlos de, 105
Lagerlöf, Selma, 46
Larkin, Philip, 74
laughter, 23, 34, 35, 43, 44, 45, 46, 49, 51, 52, 73, 74, 76, 83–84, 86, 87, 88, 100, 118, 119, 127 n.11
Leibniz, Wilhelm Gottfried von, 120
Lenbach, Franz von, 81
Le Senne, Raymond, 122 n.5
Lévi-Strauss, Claude, 19, 124 n.11, 125 n.2
Lichtenberg, Georg, 73
Limbo, 110
litotes. *See* euphemism
logic, 13, 39, 40, 48, 49, 52, 77, 81, 101, 107, 108–9, 109
love, 28, 43, 70, 87, 90, 92, 93, 97, 98, 99, 102, 112, 119

madness, *See* psychiatry
malapropism, 33, 38
man (boy), 30, 31, 38, 39, 40, 46, 49, 62, 63, 64, 69, 70, 81, 91–92, 94, 96, 102, 103
Mann, Thomas, 84, 125 n.7
Marcuse, Herbert, 30
marginality (deviants), 14, 21, 101, 107, 108, 112
marriage, 44, 59, 89, 90, 91–92, 93, 94, 95, 97, 102, 103, 104, 113
mass media, 56, 57, 60, 98
Maupassant, Guy de, 94
Maury, Philippe, 107
menstruation, 29, 30
metaphor, 95, 98, 102, 106, 111, 114, 115
Metaphysical poetry, 112
metaphysics, 14, 30, 70, 81, 83, 84, 113, 121
Minotaur, 38, 39
modern world, 32, 33, 34, 36, 96, 97, 98
monster (freak, prodigy), 14, 18, 19, 42, 43, 44, 45, 46, 48, 49, 51, 52, 58, 59, 71, 79, 104, 108, 110, 121, 123 n.1
Montaigne, Michel de, 80
music, 33, 43, 45, 75
Musset, Alfred de, 121
mutilation. *See* amputation
myth (legend), 12, 13, 20, 24, 25, 34, 38, 46, 57, 58, 59, 60, 63, 68, 98, 112, 115

name, 42, 45, 56, 58, 69, 73, 124 n.1, 127 n.11
narcissism, 17, 26, 47, 63, 69
narration, 14, 21, 22, 26, 27, 51, 57, 62, 63, 64, 65, 66, 69, 71, 82–83, 92, 115, 118
Nash, Ogden, 122 n.1
nausea, 74–75, 76, 80, 93
necrophilia. *See* perversion
neologism, 42, 48, 52, 84, 85, 108, 112, 122 n.1, 127 n.23
Nietzsche, Friedrich, 84, 87, 109, 114, 120
nomadic, 18, 19, 20, 21, 65, 81, 100

nothingness, 65, 73, 74, 76, 77, 80, 82, 83, 84, 85, 87, 88
nouvelle, 12, 14, 94–95
Novalis, 87, 113, 125n.7, 127n.28
nude, 64, 71, 102, 103

ogre, 25, 32, 33, 34, 35, 38, 47, 50, 52, 53, 95
Original Sin. *See* Fall
overlap, 14, 25, 26, 27, 29, 92, 97, 107, 112, 121
oxymoron, 42, 48, 73, 79, 89, 98, 111, 118

Paradise. *See* Eden, garden
paradox, 17, 83, 109, 118
parents, 12, 27, 28, 29, 30, 31, 32, 33, 35, 36, 37, 38, 40, 43, 76, 87, 104
Paris, 20, 33, 35, 38, 104
Parmenides, 81
parody, 104
parthenogenesis (virgin birth), 18, 36
pastiche, 43, 90, 98
Perrault, Charles, 12, 32
perversion (fetishism, sadism, necrophilia, voyeurism), 14, 19, 37, 48, 50, 51, 58, 62, 70, 75, 94, 100, 102, 103, 104, 105, 106, 107, 108, 109, 112
Petit, Susan, 129–30n.6
philosophy, 14, 68, 74, 76, 78, 80, 81, 83, 87, 97–98, 113, 120
phorie, la (portage), 33, 51, 62, 100, 109
photography, 36, 62, 63, 64, 65, 66, 67, 68, 69, 70, 73, 95, 103, 107, 111–12, 114, 123n.1, 125n.2, 126n.2
plagiarism (imitation), 12, 17, 21, 60, 67, 75
Plato, 17, 18, 30, 120, 121n.3
play, 95, 105, 109, 111, 114, 119, 121
Poe, Edgar Allan, 71, 119
point of view, 46, 53
polarization, 24, 81
pornography, 91, 108, 127n.14
postmodernism, 73, 121
primary character, 19
prodigy. *See* monster
Proust, Marcel, 31, 38, 104
psychiatry (madness), 39, 48, 49, 58, 60, 99, 102, 105, 106, 107–8, 108, 118
psychoanalysis, 19, 32, 78, 93, 128n.5
psychosomatic theory, 92–93, 95, 128n.4
puberty, 26, 28, 30, 35, 43
pun, 52, 59, 60, 68, 69, 89, 90, 93, 95, 99, 107, 111–12, 112, 112–13, 113, 114, 115, 116, 119, 123n.2, 128n.3
Purdy, Anthony, 123n.5
purity, 29, 52

Queneau, Raymond, 52, 71, 85, 124n.8, 127n.23, 129n.17
quest, 14, 33

Rabelais, François, 106
radio, 55, 56, 60, 62, 125n.2
Rais, Gilles de, 74, 77, 123n.1, 125n.11
reader (receiver), 31, 51, 56, 58, 61, 71, 74, 76, 101, 105, 108, 114, 115, 116, 116–17, 120
recycling. *See* bricolage
religion, 24, 25, 36, 42, 53, 56, 58, 64, 68, 80, 82, 85, 89–90, 92, 99, 114
Renaissance, 64, 65, 66
ritual, 14, 30, 38, 39, 47, 51, 64, 96, 97, 106
Roberts, Martin, 69, 124n.11
Rosello, Mireille, 67
Rousseau, Jean-Jacques, 26, 118, 124n.5
Ruthven, K. K., 59

sadism, *See* perversion
Sartre, Jean-Paul, 53, 75, 77, 88, 103, 109, 113, 120, 121, 123n.3, 124n.9
scatology, 10, 40, 67
school. *See* education
Schubert, Franz, 77
secondary character, 19
sedentary, 18, 19, 20, 21, 27, 65, 81, 100
serio-comic, 56, 59, 79, 95, 107, 111, 114, 121
sexism, 29, 46, 92, 104
Sexton, Anne, 124n.4
sexuality (eroticism), 14, 18, 28, 30, 34, 35, 40, 41, 47, 48, 49, 50, 51–52, 55, 58, 59, 61, 70, 77, 78, 79, 80, 90,

91, 93, 94, 101, 102, 103, 104, 106, 112, 118, 124 n.7, 126 n.10, 128 n.2
Shroud of Turin, 69
signs, 55, 109, 112, 114, 121, 124 n.11
Spinoza, Baruch, 120
Starobinski, Jean, 80
Stendhal (Henri Beyle), 113, 118
stereotype. See cliché
structure, 108, 115–16
sublimation, 45, 58, 59, 64, 66, 76, 82, 107
suicide, 75, 79, 80, 84, 86, 87
Swift, Jonathan, 73
symbol, 18, 36, 37, 60, 63, 66, 78, 80, 95, 98, 105, 108, 109, 111, 114, 114–15, 115
system, 68, 76, 81, 87, 108, 114, 126 n.14

television, 33, 35, 56, 70
Theresa, Mother, 119
Theresa of Lisieux, Saint, 80, 82
Theseus, 38, 39
Thoreau, Henry David, 20
Todorov, Tzvetan, 13
Tom Thumb, 12, 32, 46
tonsillectomy, 30, 41
torture, 63, 64, 66, 70
Tournier, Michel, works of: "L'Aire du Muguet", 20, 87, 96–100, 111, 118, 120–21; "Amandine ou les deux jardins", 22, 25, 26–31, 33, 35, 38, 39, 40, 41, 43, 87, 118, 123 n.5; *Des Clefs et des serrures,* 25, 36, 52, 70, 86, 98, 119, 126 n.7, 127 n.12, 129 n.11; "Le Coq de bruyère" (story), 25, 59, 68, 70, 89–95, 118, 119, 126 n.10; *Le Coq de bruyère* (collection), 11, 12, 14, 24, 31, 55, 111, 118, 119, 129–30 n.6; "Création et prédation", 125 n.2; *Le Crépuscule des masques,* 69, 112; "Erudition et dérision", 84; "La Famille Adam", 17–21, 22, 25, 26, 27, 28, 34, 82, 115; "Le Fétichiste", 14, 51, 101–10, 118, 120; "La Fin de Robinson Crusoé", 22–23, 26, 28, 100, 115, 118; "La Fugue du petit Poucet", 23, 25, 32–36, 40, 118, 123 n.2; *Gaspard, Melchior et Balthazar,* 11; *Gilles et Jeanne,* 11, 120, 123 n.1; *La Goutte d'or,* 11, 120, 125 n.8, 128 n.5; "Je suis un métèque de la littérature", 106; "La Jeune Fille et la mort", 25, 73–88, 89, 98, 114, 116, 118, 119, 120, 125 n.9, 128 n.5; *Journal de voyage au Canada,* 108, 128 n.8; "Journal extime (suite)", 40, 128 n.1; *Le Médianoche amoureux,* 11; "La Mère Noël", 22, 24–25, 26, 34, 118; *Les Météores,* 18, 27, 34, 52, 67, 71, 95, 108, 109, 111, 119, 120, 121, 125 n.10, 126 n.1, 129 n.8; *Miroirs,* 69; "Les Mots sous les mots", 82, 114; "Le Nain rouge", 11, 36, 42, 46–54, 55, 60, 70, 87, 108, 111, 115, 117, 118, 124 n.10; *Petites proses,* 113; "Que ma joie demeure", 34, 42–45, 51, 61, 73, 82, 118; *Le Roi des aulnes,* 40, 51, 52, 53, 62, 68, 77, 95, 106, 109, 112, 112–13, 114, 125 n.4; "Les Suaires de Véronique", 25, 42, 58, 60, 62–72, 87, 94, 115, 118, 120, 121, 122 n.1, 123 n.1; *Le Tabor et le Sinaï,* 67, 114; "Tristan Vox", 42, 55–61, 62, 63, 70, 71, 100, 116, 118, 119; "Tupik", 25, 28, 37–41, 61, 103, 116, 118; *Le Vagabond immobile,* 27, 49, 98, 127 n.20; "Variations sadiques", 71, 114; *Vendredi ou les limbes du Pacifique,* 22, 49, 109, 113, 114, 126 n.6; *Le Vent Paraclet,* 13, 22, 34, 46, 50, 52, 53, 55, 60, 73, 76, 81, 83, 84, 87, 94, 103, 106, 109, 110, 112, 116, 125 n.7, 126 n.5, 128 n.2, 128 n.5; *Le Vol du vampire,* 12, 13, 26, 49, 60, 85, 87, 88, 113, 120, 125 n.7, 129 n.4; "Les Voyages initiatiques", 88; *Vues de dos,* 53
transcendence, 88, 95
travel, 35, 96, 97, 98, 100
trees, 32, 33, 34, 35, 36, 123 n.3
Tristram and Isolde, 12, 56, 59, 60
twins, 18, 120

Valéry, Paul, 65, 88
Veronica, Saint, 12, 67, 69, 72
Vesalius, Andreas, 65, 66
vocation, 29
voluntarism, 83, 93, 103, 109, 110
voyeurism, See perversion

Weightman, John, 71, 107, 119
witch, 63, 65, 68
Wittgenstein, Ludwig, 82
woman (girl), 18, 19, 24, 25, 29, 30, 31, 33, 35, 37, 48, 49, 55, 56, 59, 60, 62, 63, 64, 69, 70, 73, 76, 81, 87, 89–90, 91, 92, 96, 100, 102, 106, 107
wordplay, 60, 95, 107, 111, 114, 115, 119
Worton, Michael, 45, 116
wounds, 29, 56, 71